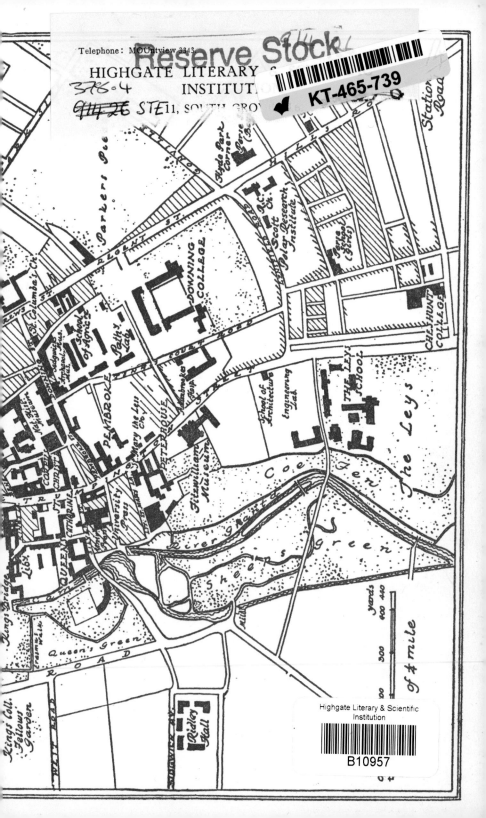

CAMBRIDGE

By the Same Author

THE RULE OF TASTE

JOSHUA REYNOLDS

HOURS IN THE NATIONAL PORTRAIT
GALLERY

THE ICONOGRAPHY OF THE DUKE OF
WELLINGTON (WITH LORD GERALD
WELLESLEY)

CONSORT OF TASTE

1   Trinity Hall and King's Old Court (from Ackermann's *Cambridge*)

CAMBRIDGE

By

JOHN STEEGMAN

REVISED BY BRYAN LITTLE

LONDON

B. T. BATSFORD LTD.

First published, December 1940
Fifth Edition, revised, 1954

MADE AND PRINTED IN GREAT BRITAIN BY
WILLIAM CLOWES AND SONS, LIMITED, LONDON AND BECCLES
FOR THE PUBLISHERS

B. T. BATSFORD LTD

4 FITZHARDINGE STREET, PORTMAN SQUARE,
LONDON, W.I

PREFACE

PART I, CONSISTING OF CHAPTERS I TO VI, TRACES THE GROWTH of the University and Colleges, approaching the subject from the historic standpoint. I have drawn extensively on Cooper's *Annals* and Gunning's *Reminiscences* as must all writers on Cambridge. Fuller's *History of the University*, 1655, and Cole's *Collections relating to the University*, 1740, are two other authorities of almost equal importance.

Part II, consisting of Chapters VII to XI, describes the colleges, university buildings and town churches as they now appear, approaching the subject this time from the architectural standpoint. I have been helped inestimably by Willis and Clarke's great *Architectural History of Cambridge* and am also indebted to the admirable series of articles on the colleges in *Country Life*. Other valuable sources are Loggan's *Cantabrigia Illustrata*, 1688; Harraden's *Views*, 1800–30; and Ackermann's famous *History of the University*, 1815.

Part III, Chapters XII to XIV, describes the Cambridge of to-day and tries to forecast that of to-morrow.

Each college is therefore discussed in both Part I and Part II. In a few cases, the chronological order of foundation has been ignored; Clare, St. Catharine's and Sidney Sussex, for examples, are discussed in Chapters X and XI, for which alone their buildings are appropriate, rather than in Chapters I, II and III, which are appropriate to the dates of their inception. In addition, King's and Trinity are discussed for a third time in Chapter XI, by reason of their important nineteenth-century buildings.

J. S.

October, 1940.

PREFACE TO FIFTH EDITION

IN revising this book, I have in the main confined myself, while working within the general plan first conceived by its author, to the correction and better defining of points of fact. Style, manner, and artistic judgment, being essentially subjective and varying from author to author, I have left unaltered. It has, however, been necessary to make numerous changes in the chapters which deal with pre-Reformation Cambridge, and towards the end of the book the chapters on twentieth-century Cambridge life, and on its future as foreseen in the 1940s, have presented considerable problems of their own. The additions which I have made elsewhere in the book, and particularly the wholly new section on developments

v

since 1945, in any case made it essential to make reductions by way of compensation. So I felt that the modern section and the passage on the early days of the women's colleges were the most suitable places for somewhat drastic abridgment. Not being confident of my prophetic powers, and because I felt that any further forecast of the course of Cambridge life might soon be disproved, I have entirely dropped the chapter entitled " Cambridge of the Future." The book itself has therefore been rearranged in two sections instead of three.

Artistic judgment has been left, as I have already mentioned, in the form in which it has been shrewdly expressed by Mr. Steegman. He and I are in any case at one in many of our opinions, over Waterhouse, for instance, and the inspissate gloom of Whewell's dreary courts. I am, however, less enthusiastic than Mr. Steegman over Wilkins' Gothic and over the Palladian refacers of mediæval courts ; Georgian work conceived *ab initio* is, of course, a different matter— witness Gibbs' Senate House.

The comparative reader of this and earlier editions will notice that I have made some additions where buildings which seem to me important have been lightly passed over or wholly omitted. The University Church, St. Andrew's the Less, the Sturbridge Leper Chapel, and Bodley's important All Saints' Church come under this heading, and I hope that the passage on the work of Morley Horder and Eric Gill at Jesus will not be construed as undue favour to my own college. I have also felt it of urgency to equip the book with a short bibliography.

My warm thanks are due to many who have helped me in the task which I have undertaken. In my own college I owe a very special debt of gratitude to Dr. F. Brittain and Dr. F. J. E. Raby ; without their preliminary survey the work could hardly have been attempted. I also have to thank Mr. C. H. Wilson, M.A., of Jesus College. In King's I have had valuable assistance from the Librarian (Mr. A. N. L. Munby, M.A.) and from the Bursar (Mr. R. E. Macpherson, M.A.). The Bursars of Peterhouse (Air Vice-Marshal C. E. W. Lockyer), Christ's (Mr. T. C. Wyatt, M.A.), and Downing (Mr. J. Grantham, M.A.), and the Junior Bursar of Trinity (Dr. J. R. G. Bradfield) have all given most useful help, whether by correspondence or by personally showing me new work in their colleges. I also have to thank the Chaplain of St. Edward's Church (Rev. R. S. Dawson, M.A.), the Librarians of St. John's (Mr. F. B. White, M.A.) and Selwyn (Mr. J. K. St. Joseph, M.A.), and Mr. Graham Storey, M.A., and Rev. A. P. Tremlett, M.A., of Trinity Hall. I also owe a debt of gratitude, for this as for other help given, to members of the staffs of the University Libraries at Cambridge and Bristol.

B. D. G. L.
Clifton, Bristol, February, 1954

CONTENTS

ACKNOWLEDGMENT

THE Author and Publishers must acknowledge their obligation to the following sources for the photographs which illustrate this book : *Country Life*, for fig. 61 ; J. Dixon-Scott, F.R.P.S., for figs. 8, 9, 32, 33, 40, 44, 79, 82, 95, 97 and 98 ; Dorien Leigh Ltd., for figs. 80 and 87 ; Herbert Felton, F.R.P.S., for figs. 5, 6, 14, 15, 19–21, 25, 27, 28, 38, 39, 41, 43, 51, 52, 57, 64, 70, 73, 75, 89, 91 and 92 ; A. F. Kersting, F.R.P.S., for figs. 4, 7, 10, 13, 16, 18, 22, 23, 26, 29, 34–6, 45, 47–50, 53, 55, 56, 58–60, 65–9, 71, 72, 74, 77, 78, 83, 90, 93 and 94 ; The Mustograph Agency, for figs. 11 and 12 ; *Picture Post*, for figs. 2 and 85 ; Ramsey and Muspratt, Cambridge, for figs. 30, 37, 63, 86 and 88 ; Sport & General Press Agency Ltd., for fig. 3 ; the late Will F. Taylor, for figs. 24, 31, 42, 54, 62 and 96 ; *The Times*, for fig. 76.

Special thanks are due to the authorities of the Fitzwilliam Museum and of the Cambridge Public Library for their help in providing illustrations and permitting their reproduction in these pages ; also to W. Heffer and Sons Ltd., Cambridge, for their advice and for the loan of blocks.

A BOOK LIST

A COMPLETE Cambridge bibliography would be far beyond the scope and compass of this book, but I have thought it desirable to compile, for this revised edition, a list of some of the essential works, whether historical, architectural, or descriptive of Cambridge life, which are available up to 1953. I have added a list of college histories, in most cases confining myself to one book for each college. Thomas Fuller, *The History of the University of Cambridge*, 1655, also edited by Prickett and Wright, 1840. William Cole, *Collections Relating to the University*, 1740. George Dyer, *History of the University and Colleges of Cambridge*, 1814. Charles Cooper, *Annals of Cambridge*, 4 vols., 1842–52, vol. v, ed. by J. Willis Clark, 1908. Henry Gunning, *Reminiscences of . . . Cambridge from the year 1780*, 2 vols., 1854. James Bass Mullinger, *The University of Cambridge*, 3 vols., 1873, 1884, and 1911. For the more general question of University History, see Hastings Rashdall, *The Universities of Europe in the Middle Ages*, ed. F. M. Powicke and A. B. Emden, 3 vols., 1936. Important works for the town (now city) and University of Cambridge are two by Arthur Gray, *The Town of Cambridge*, 1925, and *Cambridge University*, 1926. See also J. Willis Clark, *Cambridge*, 1907. More specialist works, of great value, are F. W. Maitland, *Township and Borough*, 1898, and Cyril Fox, *The Archaeology of the Cambridge Region*, 1923. Another general work is M. A. R. Tuker's *Cambridge*, 1907. Other works of a more detailed character are D. A. Winstanley, *The University of Cambridge in the Eighteenth Century*, 1922, *Unreformed Cambridge*, 1935, *Early Victorian Cambridge*, 1940, and *Later Victorian Cambridge*, 1947, and S. C. Roberts, *A History of the Cambridge University Press*, 1921. For the University Church see W. D. Bushell, *The Church of St. Mary the Great*, 1948. Valuable material can be gleaned from the *Victoria County History* of Cambridgeshire and from the publications of the Cambridge Antiquarian Society.

Books with a bearing on Cambridge life and society include Arthur Shipley, *Cambridge Cameos*, 1924, T. R. Glover, *A Cambridge Retrospect*, 1943, A. S. F. Gow, *Letters from Cambridge*, 1945, Florence Ada Keynes, *By Ways of Cambridge History*, 1947, Gwen Raverat, *Period Piece, A Cambridge Childhood*, 1952, and L. T. Stanley, *Life in Cambridge*, 1953. For description and architecture see Loggan, *Cantabrigia Illustrata*, 1688, Ackermann's *History of the University of Cambridge*, 1815, and R. B. Harraden, *Picturesque Views of Cambridge*, 1800, and *Illustrations of the University of Cambridge*, 1830. The indispensable authority is, of course, R. Willis and

A BOOK LIST

J. Willis Clark, *Architectural History of the University and Colleges of Cambridge*, 4 vols., 1886. Much of its material is contained, in shorter form, in T. D. Atkinson and J. Willis Clark, *Cambridge Described and Illustrated*, 1897. Very valuable material is also to be found in the articles on the University and Colleges which long appeared in *Country Life*; they can be tracked from the cumulative index in the bound volumes. See also T. Fyfe, *Architecture in Cambridge*, 1942, and a valuable appreciation of Cambridge's Renaissance architecture by A. E. Richardson in the *Reports and Papers* of the Northamptonshire Architectural and Archæological Society, 1942. Some of the most modern work is also covered by J. M. Richards in the *Architectural Review*, August, 1952. See also W. Holford and H. Myles Wright, *Cambridge: Planning Proposals*, 2 vols., 1950.

College Histories : Peterhouse, T. A. Walker, 1906. Clare, *Clare College*, 1326–1926, 2 vols., 1928 and 1930. Pembroke, Aubrey Attwater, 1936. Gonville and Caius, John Venn, 1901. Trinity Hall, H. E. Malden, 1902. Corpus Christi, H. P. Stokes, 1898, and, for the period 1822–1952, J. P. Bury, 1952. King's, A. Austen Leigh, 1899, and C. R. Fay, 1907. Queens', J. H. Gray, 1926, and C. T. Seltman, 1951. St. Catharine's, W. H. S. Jones, 1936 and 1951. Jesus, A. Gray, 1902. Christ's, J. Peile, 1898 and for the period up to 1508, A. H. Lloyd, 1934. St. John's, J. B. Mullinger, 1901, and R. F. Scott, 1907. Magdalene, E. K. Purnell, 1904. Trinity, G. M. Trevelyan, 1943. Emmanuel, E. S. Shuckburgh, 1904. Sidney Sussex, G. M. Edwards, 1899. Downing, H. P. W. Stevens, 1899. Selwyn, A. L. Brown, 1906. Girton, Barbara Stephen, 1933. Newnham, Alice Gardner, 1921, and Mary Agnes Hamilton, 1936.

February, 1954   B. D. G. L.

2 Proctor and Bull-dogs

3   St. John's : the Main Gate

PART I HISTORY

I Mediæval Cambridge

THE UNIVERSITY OF CAMBRIDGE WAS NOT FOUNDED BY AN Iberian Prince called Cantaber. It was not, indeed, founded by anybody, though it has any number of improbable legendary origins, many of which have fictitious Royal Charters or Papal Bulls behind them.

Even to-day Cambridge does not, by reason of its climate, seem the most eligible place in the world in which to have established a University. In the Middle Ages it must have been yet more ineligible. On the edge of the Fens, an immense tract of bog, morass, and marshy lakes, it was subject to repeated and disastrous flooding, and it might well be thought that if a University were to grow up in the eastern Midlands it would have chosen Northampton, Peterborough, or Stamford, all of which were monastic or mendicant seats of learning.

It is evident that there must have been reasons, though it is doubtful if any conscious act of selection ever took place. In Roman times Cambridge was in the centre of the country of the Iceni, once ruled over by Boadicea. The Roman roads from Colchester to Chester, and from north-east Norfolk to south-west Wales, skirting the Fens, passed through it and, as *Camboritum*, it was an important military station. Relics of the Roman occupation have been unearthed at Grantchester, Chesterton, Sawston, Shelford, Trumpington, Wimpole, Harston, in Cambridge itself, and on the Gogmagog Hills.

The Roman *Camboritum* and its Saxon successor Grantebrigge were on the left bank of the river Cam—the side now associated with the Backs. Domesday records that the Borough of Grantebrigge then consisted of about 370 houses, of which some fifty were ruinous or decayed, besides twenty-seven which had been demolished to make room for the Castle. In the meantime a considerable pre-Conquest township had grown up on the right, or East Anglian side of the river,[1] and this community across the Cam was later given additional stimulus by the establishment, about 1112, of the Augustinian Priory of Barnwell, its canons having originally been established, by the Norman Sheriff Picot, in the parish of St. Giles on the same side of the river as the Castle.

It must not be forgotten that the infant growth both of Cambridge and Oxford may well have been conditioned by ascetic and monastic ideas. The Fens, with their ready appeal to the ideal of asceticism and their plenitude of " Scenes of Horror," were admirable for monastic seclusion, and at least four major monasteries grew up in their wastes—Ely, Croyland, Ramsey, and Thorney. Cambridge, a place of military importance under the Normans as it had been under the Romans, may have seemed suitable as a place of learning. At some time during the twelfth century Cambridge did establish itself as such a place, and began to attract students and teachers.

At the same time the town itself was developing, and at the end of the century King John paid a good deal of attention to it. He began by exacting 250 marks from its burgesses in 1199, but he did in another two years compensate them by confirming their privilege of having a Guild of Merchants. About 1211 he granted to the Leper Hospital at Stourbridge, beyond Barnwell, a fair which became famous all over Europe as the Stourbridge Fair. This was made over to the Corporation after the Dissolution of the Hospital. Like many of his mediæval successors on the throne, John paid repeated visits to Cambridge, but seems never to have stayed in the Castle. Edward I, in 1293, was probably the first King to do that, and even then he gave his fifty horses the privilege of being stabled at Barnwell Priory. John stayed generally at Barnwell, instead of the Castle, but the prior of that house was not by any means the only dignitary to feel the weight of the royal presence. Because it was the King's property, the Sheriff was ordered to repair the Castle, and the Abbot of Ramsey was made to convey fish to Barnwell for consumption by the King and court on Ash Wednesday, 1206. The fishponds and meres round Ramsey were certainly well stocked with perch, roach, pike, eels, and the much-favoured lampreys, but King John and his court were probably a severe drain even on the teeming Fens.

To turn from the growing borough to the infant University, we find but scant material relating to the period before the foundation of the earliest colleges. All that can be said is that during the

---

[1] For a valuable article on early Cambridge, taking other authorities such as Maitland into full account, see Helen M. Cam on " The Origin of the Borough of Cambridge " in *Liberties and Communities of Mediæval England*, 1944, pp. 1–18.— B.D.G.L.

4   Peterhouse, from the Fellows' Garden

5   Corpus : the Old Court

6   Trinity Hall : the Library

7   Trinity Hall : the Library

8 Corpus Christi and St. Botolph's Church, from Trumpington Street

9 Pembroke, from Trumpington Street

10   Peterhouse : the Chapel, with the Fellows' Building beyond

thirteenth century Cambridge was gradually becoming a centre of learning. The students lived at their own cost in lodging-houses, or in hostels under the rule of Principals. This at least offered some security, but their teaching had to be obtained from any master who could collect a sufficient body of students, or from the various mendicant friars. A major aim of these latter was, of course, recruiting for their particular Orders, and not unnaturally they had considerable success among the inexperienced, impoverished, and studious youths, many of them of about fourteen, who were the earliest undergraduates.

The Hospital of St. John the Evangelist, probably founded about 1200 [1] under the management of a body of priests following the " Rule " of St. Augustine, is among the earliest of the establishments which gave lodging to students during the thirteenth century. The earliest college, Peterhouse, was not founded till 1284. The history of the eight decades between these dates is obscure, but two facts at any rate are clear.

The first is the migration of a number of students from Paris to Oxford. Paris, even more than Bologna, was the intellectual centre of Europe during the twelfth century, but it began to decline before the end of the thirteenth. Then in 1209 some students migrated from Oxford, in consequence of the already recurrent town-and-gown disputes, and settled in Cambridge. It must at once be observed that the poor creatures were not fortunate in their choice, for the town-and-gown rows in Cambridge were carried on with a ferocity and frequency enough to dismay even the toughest *emigré* from Paris or Oxford. The worst rows, however, occurred during the fourteenth century, when colleges were being founded and when the University was well established in wealth and privilege.

The second circumstance is the growth of conventual houses in and on the outskirts of the town. The Priory of Barnwell was the first, as we have seen, and remained till the dissolution the largest, wealthiest, and most important of them all. Soon after 1130 the Benedictine Nunnery of St. Radegund was founded and its buildings became, in due course, those of Jesus College ; the earlier buildings of St. Radegund's seem repeatedly to have fallen down, been burnt to the ground, or severely damaged by tempests, so that the nuns can have been in little danger of insufficient mortification. About a century passed before the next conventual foundation. Some time between 1221 and 1238 came the foundation of the Dominican Friary whose site became that of Emmanuel. The Franciscans, eventually settled on the site of Sidney Sussex, were founded by 1232.

[1] See Victoria County History of Cambridgeshire, Vol. II, 1948.—B.D.G.L.

Shortly after 1250 the Carmelites (White Friars) settled at Newnham, moving by the end of the century to their site on the right bank of the Cam immediately behind the site of the later Queens' College. The Friars of the Penitence of Jesus (or of the Sack) were for some years in the parish of St. Peter's the Less on the site of Peterhouse, and the Augustinian Friars were settled before 1300 in a large Friary on the site of the Arts School. In 1278 Cambridge was a fair-sized town, as towns went in those days, and contained no fewer than nine religious houses and seventeen parish churches, later enumerated in an Inquisition of Edward III.

Both town and University were growing fast. The town, like Oxford, contained many rich Jews who, in common with their Christian fellow-citizens, had been much harassed by the rebellious barons, known as " The Disinherited," who had captured the Isle of Ely in 1266. The unfortunate Prior of Barnwell was also victimised by these survivors of de Montfort's party, as his predecessor had been by John, for their raiding parties descended daily upon the Priory, eating and drinking what they pleased and insulting the Prior. These barons also carried off for ransom most of the richer Jews, and Henry III, probably with a view to the future replenishing of his Treasury, proclaimed that no one, under penalty of death or torture, should molest the Jews in Cambridge.

The University had achieved some of its full status some thirty years before this, though it was not recognised by the Pope as a *Studium Generale* till 1318. The first recorded Chancellor was Hugh de Hottun, elected in or before 1246.[1] A Charter of Henry III regulated both civic and academic life in Cambridge, threatening severe penalties on both laymen and clerks who should molest one another, and in 1275 a Congregation consisting of the Chancellor, the Masters Regent and non-Regent and the Bachelors of the University took place in Great St. Mary's Church, disciplinary statutes being laid down in the pious hope that they would ensure peace for the University. Government was vested in the Chancellor and in the Houses of Regents (Teachers) and of non-Regents (non-Teachers), who divided between them the functions of teaching and administration.

All this was still before the era of colleges. The University existed many years before any individual colleges came into being, and University statutes preceded, though not by many years, college statutes. The corporate bodies called colleges are, and always have been, quite distinct from the corporate body called the University ; they are self-governing and to a large extent independent of Uni-

[1] Baker MSS, University Library.—B.D.G.L.

4

11   Clare : Gates leading from the Backs

12   Caius : looking through the Gate of Virtue

13   King's : the Chapel, looking East

versity control, but since practically all members of the University are members of some college it is quite impossible nowadays to imagine one existing without the other.

Before entering on the era of the colleges, we may dwell for a moment on the matter of town-and-gown rows, which existed before that era and continued well and noisily into it, and indeed into the eighteenth century at least. The chief trouble seems to have been jealousy on the part of the town at the growing immunities from taxation and the privileges enjoyed by the " clerks." There was also a deep mistrust, on the part of the common people, of learning as such, but this hardly ever became articulate without being given a lead. It always was given a lead, generally by the mayor himself.

We have seen how a body of students left Oxford for Cambridge in 1209 because of these disturbances. By 1240 Cambridge itself had so many that Henry III addressed the sheriff of the county very sharply on the subject. Then in 1261 a number of peace-loving scholars from both Universities tried, despairingly, to found a third and more restful University at Northampton, but were very soon ordered home by the King. Another attempt of the same kind, this time at Stamford, was made in 1334 with the same humiliating result. These riots were more or less endemic, but they occasionally became sufficiently grave to have been specially recorded, as in 1304, 1322, 1334, and, the most memorable of all, in 1381, when a mob led by the mayor and burgesses broke open and sacked most of the hostels and destroyed all the Bulls, Charters, and Muniments in the University chest. All the Statutes and Ordinances were publicly burnt in the market-place, amid shouts of " Away with the skill of the Clerks ! " This particular riot goes a long way towards explaining the obscurity of early University history.

One enduring feature of past and present University life makes its appearance about 1340—the pleasant habit of gay, unorthodox clothes. The young persons of the fourteenth century rightly felt that a little affectation became their adolescent years, but, as always, they were severely censured for it. Great complaint was made against their unclerical apparel ; that instead of the tonsure they wore their hair long, curled and scented ; that they wore furred cloaks, brightly coloured shoes, and extravagantly long, hanging sleeves ; that their fingers were decorated with rings and their waists encircled with jewelled girdles. These breaches of decorum were viewed in the worst possible light and regarded as disqualification for any degree. It probably made not an atom of difference to the " rich set " of the fourteenth century.

Now we must go back to the rise of individual colleges, beginning in 1284 with Peterhouse. This was founded by Hugh de Balsham, Bishop of Ely, one of the most enlightened of all Cambridge benefactors. His original scheme had been to modify the existing Hospital of St. John by endowing a number of secular scholars in common with the " religious " brethren. This attempt was foiled almost entirely by the canons' jealousy of the secular scholars, so that Bishop Hugh was compelled to withdraw these latter and endow them separately as St. Peter's College, or Peterhouse. Twenty-five years later, in 1309, the college was further enriched, and its immediate site enlarged, by coming into possession of the property of the suppressed Friary of the Penitence of Jesus. Quite a number of colleges owe either their foundation or a great increase in their wealth to the suppression of some other religious house, but this is the earliest instance.

Hugh de Balsham in founding Peterhouse had in mind the great foundation of Walter de Merton at Oxford, but it was really one of his successors at Ely, Simon de Montacute, who in 1338 laid down the statutes of the college, which were closely copied from those of Merton College, in which clear expression was given to the founder's intention that the college was to be non-monastic in character. Neither Hugh de Balsham nor Simon de Montacute had intended any hostility to the monastic orders, but it was nevertheless a shrewd and useful hit at the pretensions and powers of the monks. It was made perfectly clear that the college was intended to help students without their being under the necessity of embracing the monastic life, and it was emphatically not the founder's idea to provide a home for monks.

The next collegiate foundation was not till 1317, when Edward II made a start with the foundation of King's Hall which was later augmented and enriched by his son Edward III.[1] Then in 1324 Hervey de Stanton founded Michaelhouse. Both of these foundations were subsequently incorporated in Trinity College.

The fourteenth century produced five colleges which still survive. Founded in 1347, Pembroke is nearly opposite Peterhouse on the other side of Trumpington Street. The College of Valence Marie, or Pembroke Hall as it was long called, owes its existence to the illustrious Marie de St. Pol, daughter of the Comte de Chatillon and widow of the great Aymer de Valence, Earl of Pembroke. He is erroneously said to have been killed in a tourney on his wedding day, which explains Gray's reference in his " Installation Ode " :—

> . . . sad Chatillon, on her bridal morn
> That wept her bleeding love.

[1] See G. M. Trevelyan, *Trinity College*, 1943, p. 3.—B.D.G.L.

Although Pembroke has in recent years been much concerned with the production of Rugby blues, it also has an illustrious academic and literary record, particularly in the sixteenth century, when Edmund Spenser and Gabriel Harvey waged some of the most important and epoch-making battles in English literary history, and in the eighteenth century when shy, quiet, ugly, scholarly Gray enriched the language with his exquisitely fastidious poetry. The ecstatic Crashaw was also a product of this college of poets.

The year after Pembroke's foundation saw the establishment of Gonville Hall, later to be refounded as Gonville and Caius College. It was originally situated in Freeschool Lane, near Corpus Christi College. Edmund Gonville himself was a member of an old Norfolk family, and since he was also a parson his design had a strong bias towards theology and was based on the desire to encourage learning in his own profession. It seems evident enough that the level of learning had sunk pretty low both in the University and in the professions outside it, for in the early statutes of Pembroke Hall it had been necessary to provide for instruction in Latin.

Trinity Hall, still called Trinity Hall and with no connection whatever with Trinity College, was founded in 1350 by William Bateman as a direct result of the Black Death. Bateman was Bishop of Norwich, and contemplated with dismay the heavy mortality among the clergy in his diocese through that appalling pestilence. He founded his college with the express purpose of ensuring a steady supply of young men who were highly trained in civil and canon law; many of these would be priests who would serve in parishes. Bateman showed, both in Cambridge and at Norwich, a good deal of that go-ahead spirit which made him one of the Pope's most valuable organisers at Avignon. He died there in 1355, and the cup which he gave to the College by his will is still in their possession.

Corpus Christi College also, in a sense, owes its origin to the Black Death. One of the results of that visitation was that, owing to the heavy mortality among the clergy, the fees asked for the celebration of private requiem masses had risen to an exorbitant level. It therefore occurred to the two civic Guilds of Corpus Christi and the Blessed Virgin to found a college for the educating of clergy who should be compelled to celebrate masses for the souls of any departed members of either Guild.[1] In this businesslike manner, in 1352, Corpus came into existence.

An earlier college foundation of the fourteenth century was Clare Hall, eventually, like Pembroke, Christ's, St. John's, Queens', and

[1] The Guilds amalgamated for the purpose of founding the College.—B.D.G.L.

Sidney, the creation of an august benefactress. It was originally founded, in 1326, by the University itself, as University Hall. It was not a success, so in 1338 it came under the protection of Elizabeth de Burgh, granddaughter of Edward I, sister and coheiress of Gilbert de Clare, Earl of Gloucester, who had been killed at Bannockburn. She refounded and renamed it, and in 1359 she gave the College statutes in which she referred to the need to make up losses among the clergy occasioned by the Black Death.

After Corpus, no other college was founded till King's in 1441. Peterhouse and Clare had repetitions, or at least adaptations, of the statutes of Merton. Gonville and Trinity Halls were training colleges, in the manner approved by the Papal administration at Avignon. Corpus represented the feelings of pious laymen with a definite *arrière-pensée*. Whatever may be true of the generality of Oxford founders, by no means all the Cambridge colleges owe their existence, in their present form, to churchmen. The founders include monarchs and their consorts, noble ladies, merchants, an occasional county magnate, and comparatively few bishops.

While the Colleges were thus increasing in numbers, the old original hostels continued their rather ramshackle existence, and indeed their inmates long constituted the greater part of the University. Then in addition there were students of a separate group—the " glomerels," or grammar students.[1] These students, under their own " Master of Glomery " and their separate schoolhouse, were characterised by their poverty, their extreme youth (they were generally about fourteen or fifteen), and extreme lack of ambition, their sole aim being as a rule to acquire just enough Latin to qualify as schoolmasters. On becoming a " Master in Grammar " a former student was entitled to signify his new dignity by publicly whipping in the Schools a boy selected for this purpose by the Bedell. From the beginning of the thirteenth century onwards the humble grammar student played a very inferior part to the arts student, whose course included logic, mathematics, and rhetoric as well as canon and civil law. The form of instruction was, of course, the Lecture and the Public Disputation.

A notable intention of the early colleges is the intention to help the poor student, and in fact the University was designed principally for such. Even to-day the discomfort in some of the older rooms in any college is quite considerable ; in the fourteenth century it must have been appalling, and the average boy was probably often on the border of starvation.

[1] See Arthur Gray, *Cambridge University*, 1926, pp. 27–8 and 55–7.—B.D.G.L.

II   Renaissance Cambridge

THE EARLY GROWTH OF THE UNIVERSITY WAS CERTAINLY to some extent conditioned by the monastic ideal in general and by the Cambridge conventual houses in particular. But by the beginning of the fifteenth century monasticism was far from being what at one time it had been. Opposition to the system was pretty general, officially led by the great Wyclif in Oxford, and soon both Cambridge and Oxford became centres of Lollardism : partly the extreme left-wing Lollardism that would be quite at home in any Union debate to-day, partly a more academic " pink " socialism rather in the London School of Economics manner. Thomas Arundel, Archbishop of Canterbury, descended in full state upon Cambridge in 1401 and subjected the Chancellor, Doctors, and Masters to a questioning on the matter of Lollardry which, in view of the quite recent Statute *De Hæretico Comburendo*, must have alarmed them considerably. Nevertheless, though the University did not become the headquarters of left-wing thought, it was able to free itself more and more from ecclesiastical control, despite occasional attempts by Bishops of Ely to assert their traditional authority and exact the oath of canonical obedience from the Chancellor.

Learning was departing from the monasteries and the friaries, but till near the end of the fifteenth century, despite Henry VI, it was not very notably settling anywhere else. The French Wars and the squalid civil struggle oddly known as the Wars of the Roses had as demoralising an effect on the Universities as they had on most other things in that obscure century, and not until the coming of the great Humanists at the end of the century does the real Renaissance begin.

Archbishop Arundel's Inquisition of 1401 clamped down severely on the progressive element, and twenty years later obscurantism was given further encouragement by an enactment restraining the practice of physic throughout England to those who had graduated in that faculty in the two Universities.

3   9

However, the outstanding event in Cambridge in the fifteenth century is the foundation of King's College by the pious, learned and in this case very methodical Henry VI. The king here followed the example of William of Wykeham and his twin foundations of Winchester and New College, Oxford. Henry's counterpart to Winchester is Eton. The revenues of these two came from a very large number of suppressed alien priories, that is, English cells of foreign monastic houses, whose property had been confiscated during the Hundred Years War.

The King's College of Our Lady and St. Nicholas began its richly endowed existence in 1441. For a hundred years King's remained by far the richest college in the university, and for a great deal longer than that it remained the most unpopular. There were, indeed, many causes of jealousy : its great wealth, the privileges granted by the king with papal and parliamentary sanction, and its immunity from University control. In fact, from the very beginning King's tended to regard itself as separate from other colleges at least in degree if not in kind.

The great Chapel was planned by the king in the most minute detail. Although it was begun in his reign, the civil wars soon put a stop to it. This great church, dominating the little town, was not just intended to be the chapel of a Provost and seventy scholars. It was not only intended to be a monument to the Glory of God, of Our Lady, and of St. Nicholas, or to the piety of King Henry, but it was also and above all a witness to the Glory of the Church herself, the ultramontane, conservative Mother Church, a princely reprimand to all Lollards and questioners. Its foundation stone was laid by the king in person in 1446. The King's plans also included a cemetery to the west of the chapel. This was to be surrounded by a cloister, and a great bell tower was to stand in the middle of the cloister's western side.

At that time a thoroughfare called Milne Street ran roughly parallel with King's Parade, or Trumpington Street, and the river. Trinity Hall and Clare both opened off it and it ran across the site of the modern King's, being to-day represented by Queens' Lane. All the area between Trumpington Street and Milne Street was covered by shops, houses, gardens, hostels, and the Church of St. John Zachary. All this the king bought up and cleared for his new college, but it was 400 years before the college occupied more than a minute corner of it.

King's is the first royal foundation in Cambridge, but a second followed very close upon it. This was Queens'—note the position of the apostrophe—founded originally in 1448 by Queen Margaret,

14　St. John's : the River Front and the " Wren " Bridge

15   St. John's :   the Second Gate from the Second Court

16   St. John's :   the Second Gate from the Third Court

the dauntless and much-suffering Consort of Henry VI. Henry was nineteen when he founded King's; Margaret was barely twenty when she addressed to her husband a petition to found a college which begins: " Besecheth mekely Margaret quene of England youre humble wif . . . " It was to have a President and four Fellows, and to-day King's and Queens' are the only Cambridge colleges not presided over by a Master; King's has its Provost, Queens' its President.

Queen Margaret's pious project, like that of her husband, wilted sadly during the civil war of the Roses. King Henry was defeated and deposed, Queen Margaret returned embittered and impoverished to her native Anjou, and the " Queen's College of St. Margaret and St. Bernard " nearly expired. It was saved by its President Andrew Doket appealing to the new queen of Edward IV, Elizabeth Wood-ville, to take the foundation under her wing. Elizabeth was the queen of a Yorkist king, but she was also the widow of a Lancastrian knight and had been a lady-in-waiting to the late Lancastrian Queen Margaret herself. So presumably she was by no means unwilling to accede to Andrew Doket's request and acquire thus the fame of a co-foundress. She gave the college its statutes, which fact explains the position of its apostrophe.

Queens' is next door to King's, appropriately enough. St. Catharine's, backing onto Queens' and now facing Trumpington Street, is the next college in date, being founded in 1473 by Robert Woodlark, Provost of King's. Perhaps the most memorable point in the genesis of St. Catharine's is that Provost Woodlark is the only man who was at the same time head of one college and founder of another.

All the colleges founded so far are reasonably close to one another. Peterhouse the farthest south, Gonville and Trinity Halls to the north, Corpus to the east, King's, Queens', St. Catharine's, and Clare all in a huddle in the middle. But the next college, Jesus, takes us at once to the other side of the town. Indeed, at that time it was beyond it to the north-east.

Jesus arose from the suppression of the twelfth-century nunnery of St. Radegund. Not only had that unfortunate convent had to face constant misfortunes, but it appears that these misfortunes in the end so undermined the discipline of the nuns that, even at the end of the fifteenth century, St. Radegund's was widely known for its corruption, laxity, and scandalous conduct. By about 1490 only two nuns remained on the foundation, so that in 1496 John Alcock, Bishop of Ely, had little difficulty in obtaining a patent from Henry VII to suppress this very ancient and at one time

11

distinguished house, and to found in its place " the College of the Blessed Virgin Mary, St. John the Evangelist, and the glorious Virgin St. Radegund, near Cambridge." [1] The present chapel is the greater part of the church of the ancient nunnery.

Archbishop Cranmer was up at Jesus and was a Fellow about 1515 ; being imprudent enough to marry the niece of the landlady of the Dolphin, a famous inn in Jesus Lane, he of course lost his fellowship. He lived with his wife at the Dolphin, and after about a year she died in childbirth, and Jesus very generously reelected him to a Fellowship. Had she lived, he would not have attained the See of Canterbury ; he would probably also have avoided the stake.

The fifteenth century passed out in the gloom and uncertainty of a post-civil-war period, with a new and by no means popular man on an uncertain throne. The Middle Ages were dead, the New Learning had hardly yet arrived at the end of its long journey from Italy, but at the very end of the century the stage was occupied at last by a man of European stature, one of the greatest of the Humanists : John Fisher. Cambridge by 1500 had entered on a new life, and just about in the nick of time.

Fisher had been a student of Michaelhouse and in 1497 had been elected Master of that College. From that date, or a few years earlier, begins his close friendship with Cambridge's most illustrious and generous benefactress—Lady Margaret Beaufort, Countess of Richmond and of Derby, descendant of Edward III and mother of Henry VII. A woman of profound piety and great wealth, burning to perform good works, she was on the point of devoting her fortune to the great Abbey of Westminster, which already possessed enormous riches, when her newly appointed chaplain, Fisher, dissuaded her from that not very intelligent course and induced her to take an interest in the University. Fisher, like his friend and admirer Erasmus, was a prophet of the New Learning, while monks, whether at Westminster or anywhere else, seemed obviously to be its enemies.

The results of Fisher's influence on the king's mother were seen first in 1503, in the foundation of the Lady Margaret Professorship of Divinity, which under the guidance of Fisher and Erasmus became an admirable vehicle for reform within a few years of its foundation. The second result was the foundation in 1505 of Christ's College, on the outskirts of the town though not so remote as Jesus. The Master of Michaelhouse had, just before this date and greatly to his own astonishment, been appointed Bishop of Rochester. Being in addition Chancellor of the University, he was quickly recognised as

[1] From a very early period it was known as Jesus College.—B.D.G.L.

17   St. John's : the Old Chapel (from Ackermann's *Cambridge*)

18   St. John's : the New Chapel

19   Queens' : the Wooden Bridge and Essex's Building

20   Queens': the President's Lodge from the Second Court

21　St. Catharine's

22　Jesus : the Entrance Gate, from the Chimney

the outstanding figure in Cambridge; his influence on behalf of the University over Lady Margaret was complete and began to extend itself over Henry VII as well, with at least one magnificent result— the completion of King's College Chapel. Ever since the accession of Edward IV the great building had remained a dreary shell, incomplete and unroofed. Considering that what small, shadowy claim Henry had to his crown came from his Lancastrian descent through his mother it is surprising that he should so long have neglected to do honour to the pious shade of his predecessor. At last, soon before his death in 1509, by an act of magnificent openhandedness very remarkable in one whose fists were notoriously tight, he made over two separate sums of £5,000 to the college for the completion of the Chapel—a gigantic benefaction, which has placed every sojourner in Cambridge from that day to this irredeemably in debt to that unlovable king.

As soon as Christ's was founded the insatiable Lady Margaret made it known that she intended to found yet another college, to be grafted onto the stock of the ancient Hospital of St. John. Unfortunately this venerable foundation had sunk so hopelessly into debt and other difficulties that there was nothing for it but dissolution and a refounding. Before the royal assent could be obtained the king died, and two months later the Lady Margaret herself followed him. Then Fisher's troubles began; difficulties with Lady Margaret's executors, difficulties with Ely, difficulties with Rome, difficulties with Canterbury, difficulties with Wolsey himself. Despite opposition and legal delays, the old Hospital was successfully suppressed and the new College of St. John the Evangelist came into being in 1511, admitting, as it still admits, Lady Margaret as its foundress, but owing its existence to John Fisher.

Fisher, in fact, is Cambridge during these opening years of the sixteenth century. A man of saintly character and a profound scholar, he showed, as Chancellor of the University for thirty years, an organising ability and a sympathy with reform that in all probability saved the university from a decline which might have led in a few years to extinction. This tight-lipped ascetic, part don, part bishop, part the old-fashioned parson, was far from being a liberal, but he was to a rather surprising extent an advocate of the New Learning. And round the question of the New Learning the whole of Cambridge was buzzing in the early years of Henry VIII. It meant really, Should Greek be taught or forbidden, should men think for themselves along new lines, probably ending up in heresy, or continue in the old footsteps of the mediæval Schoolmen?

Among the residents in Queens' from early in 1510 to the end of 1513 was Desiderius Erasmus " of Rotterdam," immortalised by his Letters, by his learning and by the brush of Holbein, but nevertheless to his contemporaries a little sharp-nosed, querulous creature, who although a Dutchman spoke no Dutch nor, indeed, a word of anything but Latin, who hated Cambridge and was avowedly there to look for a job. He complained loudly and often about Cambridge beer and imported great quantities of Burgundy, which helps a lot in explaining his chronic financial difficulties. Nevertheless, he was the first to teach Greek in Cambridge, a dangerous and novel undertaking, bringing with it at the least unpopularity and at the worst risk of persecution. And he was an early textual critic of the Bible, a hardly less dangerous undertaking. But Erasmus, most fortunately for himself, was protected by the omnipotent Fisher, and when the disgruntled Rotterodamian left the damp and misty town, which so strongly reminded him of his own detested Holland, both the study of Greek and the opposition to it were in full swing.

The opposition, however, never reached the height of violence which it achieved at Oxford. That university in 1520 had barely emerged from the Middle Ages ; the illustrious figures of Grocyn, Linacre, and Thomas More were no longer to be seen in that home of mediæval theology, so that the teaching of Greek and the consequent revolutionising of the schools had practically no support except from the distinguished Cambridge scholar, Richard Foxe of Pembroke, who in 1516 founded Corpus Christi at Oxford and made thereby an emphatic declaration in favour of the New Learning. This was the signal for the students to band themselves together as " Trojans " and to assault and insult the bewildered and inoffensive " Grecians," until in 1519 a letter from Henry VIII himself insisted that a stop be put to this nonsense. The rabble of " Trojan " undergraduates were thoroughly discomfited and Greek was established. It is pretty safe to say that if Oxford had had a Chancellor of the calibre of Fisher it would not have made itself so ridiculous.

The magnificent Cardinal Wolsey visited Cambridge in high state in 1520, but amongst the dignitaries who received him the Chancellor Fisher was not present. The Cardinal represented almost everything of which Fisher disapproved ; nevertheless, the university was determined, in spite of its austere Chancellor, to follow the example of Oxford and abase itself completely before the Cardinal. The university therefore humiliated itself as the other had done by giving up its statutes entirely and unreservedly into the Cardinal's hands, to be " reformed, corrected, changed, renewed." Wolsey was duly gratified, but his promised favours seem to have been limited to placing on his own foundation of Cardinal College in

23   Christ's : the First Court, with the Master's Lodge

24   St. John's : the Hall, from the Second Court

26   Jesus : the Cloister and Chapel Tower

25   Christ's : the Entrance Gateway

Oxford a number of the most promising young scholars from Cambridge. It is not known how this tribute to Cambridge was received by the other society.

Within ten years Wolsey was disgraced and dead ; within another five Fisher was disgraced also and executed, achieving immortal renown by his martyrdom. And Cambridge experienced the full blast of the Reformation.

III Reformation Cambridge

IT COULD BE ASSERTED, THOUGH IT MIGHT BE RASH TO DO SO, that the Reformation in England began at Cambridge. The assertion, if made, would be based on the activities of the Lady Margaret Professor of Divinity between 1511 and 1513. The professor was our expatriate Dutchman Erasmus, and there is no doubt whatever that his pupils, fired by his example, spread the new spirit of enquiry throughout the university. Both universities played important parts in the reforming movement, and by 1525 Cambridge was attracting rather a dangerous amount of attention as the centre of a revolt from the old doctrines of the divinity schools.

Fisher, though a good friend to the New Learning, was no supporter of heresy. Ecclesiastical and scholastic reform were all very well, and indeed desirable, but when it came to Martin Luther it was high time to take repressive action. Fisher, as Bishop of Rochester, preached a sermon before Wolsey denouncing the books of Luther as heretical, and as Chancellor of the University he supervised their public burning.

But this conflagration, like most such suppressions, was really all in vain. It could not prevent the famous and almost legendary meetings at the White Horse, an inn close to the site of what was once the Bull Hotel in King's Parade. Here met the Cambridge reformers and here were studied, discussed and criticised the new doctrines from Germany. The Reformers, whose White Horse meetings did not long remain secret, included Hugh Latimer, who was a Fellow of Clare ; William Tyndale, who had migrated from Oxford to escape the persecution of the " Trojan " buffoons ; and Miles Coverdale, then an inmate of the Austin Friars. The little colony of Cambridge men which Wolsey settled at his great college in Oxford was largely recruited from the White Horse set, with the result that Oxford was rapidly infected with what were, in the opinion of the Warden of New College, these pestilential new doctrines. " Would God," he exclaimed, " that his Grace had never motioned to call any Cam-

27 Trinity : the Main Gate

28 Trinity : the Great Court, looking North

bridge man to his most godly college ! We were clear without blot
till they came."

Within a year or two one of the supreme dramas of English
history deeply involved the University, and with the tragic end
of that drama Cambridge left the Middle Ages behind her for
ever.

The king divorced Katherine of Aragon, and the University, not
without some skilful hedging, declared itself not unfavourable to
this proceeding. But the Chancellor stood wholly aloof, a firm and
implacable opponent of the divorce. Cambridge, thanks to her not
very courageous handling of the tremendous situation, escaped
unscathed as subsequent events rolled on. But John Fisher went
down heroically in disaster : arrest, trial, condemnation and execution. To most men then at Cambridge he seemed to have been
guiding them and watching over them for as long as they could
remember. He is the special glory of St. John's.

A few months later Thomas Cromwell was Chancellor of the
University in the place of Fisher. The first result of this is seen in
the Royal Injunctions, which substituted the royal for the papal
authority and which completely modernised the scope of teaching
in the schools. The second result is the dissolution of the monastic
houses and friaries, from the still wealthy Barnwell downwards.
And the immediate effect of the dissolution is the great diminishing of
the resources and the numbers of the University, which by about 1540
could quite truthfully be described as being in straitened circumstances. Roger Ascham describes it as " this destitute and unhappy
university." Ascham was a member of St. John's, at this time
unquestionably the leading college in the University, including as
Fellows, besides Ascham, John Cheke, the first Regius Professor of
Greek and one of the most illustrious of Johnians, and William Cecil,
the future Lord Burghley and Chancellor, at that time a college
lecturer in Greek.

Although materially in a bad way, the University was rapidly
becoming the intellectual centre of influence, and the future of
England really seemed to be in the hands of a group of Cambridge
men. Cheke and Cecil have already been mentioned ; Roger
Ascham, a pupil of Cheke, and William Grindall, both of St. John's,
were successively tutors of Elizabeth I, and that was no light responsibility. John Aylmer was tutor of Lady Jane Grey. If the
English Reformation were not actually born in Cambridge, the
Protestant Church grew up there. And, further, Cambridge played
a very considerable part in the career of Elizabeth I herself : Ascham,
Grindall, Parker, Whitgift and Cecil were likely in the aggregate to

4*   17

keep the queen pretty well influenced by and mindful of the University that had nourished them all.

An important step towards the University's recovery was the foundation in 1540 of the five Regius Professorships of Divinity, Civil Law, Physic, Hebrew, and Greek. Henry VIII by this munificence showed himself not ungrateful to the University for its conduct in the matter of the divorce and, as was to be expected of him, a true friend to the New Learning.

When the property of the monastic houses was being confiscated by the Crown, there was included among these forfeitures in Cambridge Buckingham College. This was a hostel for Benedictine monks sent to study at Cambridge; it was in the main an offshoot of the great Abbey of Croyland, but was also used for students from other monasteries such as Ely, Ramsey, and Walden; this may be seen from the coats of arms over some of the staircases in the first court. It was bestowed, along with Walden Abbey, on Thomas, Lord Audley, and by him, in 1542, was refounded as Magdalene College. Magdalene is chiefly remarkable as the only college of ancient foundation on the left bank of the river. It is at the far northern end of the city, on the same side of the river as the Roman Camboritum, the Saxon Grantebrigge, and the great Castle of the Normans; it is also remarkable for having, unlike Magdalen, Oxford, an " e " at the end, and for having had Samuel Pepys as its most celebrated member.

But despite the Regius Professorships and the foundation of Magdalene, the University was still in a poor way, and in 1545 experienced a cause for alarm perhaps more real and threatening than anything else in its history. This was the Act for the Dissolution of Collegiate Foundations, the bulk of these, apart from the colleges at the Universities, Eton, and Winchester, being great " collegiate " churches like St. Stephen's, Westminster (dissolved) and St. George's, Windsor (specially spared). The Act was indeed passed and largely carried out, and the endowments of the colleges in both Universities were within measurable distance of going the same way as those of the monasteries. The danger was, of course, averted, but it had been a near thing, and in the case of Cambridge the compassion of the despoiler was probably moved by the intercession of John Cheke with the benevolent and virtuous Queen Catherine Parr. And it is probably also due to her that the king formed his intention " to advance learning and erect new occasion thereof," or in other words to found Trinity College, which he did in December 1546.

This royal college is an agglomeration of several earlier foundations.

18

The Master of Michaelhouse, John Fisher's old college, and the Master of King's Hall were commanded to surrender their houses into the King's hands. The buildings of the Franciscans on the eventual site of Sidney were demolished to provide building stone, and several hostels extinguished; the name of one of these hostels survives in Garret Hostel Lane, running down to the river between Trinity and Trinity Hall. It is to be observed that Henry did not find it necessary to import any scholars from Oxford on to his new foundation, having as great a faith in Cambridge scholarship as Wolsey evidently had. Trinity was, indeed, a noble neighbour to St. John's, and, together with the refounding as Christ church of Wolsey's Cardinal College, is a good and fitting end to a life and reign that so greatly helped the cause of true learning. Trinity is really Henry's best monument.

The condition of the University was rather better in 1550 than it had been ten years earlier, but there was a new element that caused a good deal of dismay and even grave dissatisfaction among the older generation. This was the prevalence of young men who were members of noble families and who came up without the smallest intention of taking a degree. The schools were deserted and the undergraduates strolled about the town in rich and gaudy clothes, frequenting the taverns and getting into debt. Roger Ascham had a good deal to say on this subject and Hugh Latimer was even more severe. From that day to this there has been a Latimer in every generation to accuse the undergraduates of idleness and dissipation; and from that day to this they have been very generally and properly ignored. But the fault, if it be a fault, lay to a large extent with the University in that nearly all the eminent men who should have taken the place of Erasmus or Fisher as teachers and inspirers were out in the larger world neglecting Cambridge. Ascham continued as Public Orator, but lived mainly abroad; John Cheke was appointed Provost of King's while absorbed in state business at court; Nicholas Ridley held the Mastership of Pembroke while Bishop of London. But one great tribute to the eminence of Cambridge scholars must be recorded; the English Prayer Book of 1549 was the work almost exclusively of Cambridge men, for twelve out of its thirteen compilers had been educated at that University.

With the death of Edward VI, Cambridge found itself suddenly in the middle of an excitement which was more than embarrassing and which it could well have dispensed with. The Duke of Northumberland had proclaimed as queen his daughter-in-law, Lady Jane Grey; Mary, the late king's sister, hurried off to safety at Sawston Hall, near Cambridge, but soon had to make her escape from there in disguise to avoid the Protestant citizens of Cambridge, who marched out to attack the house. She fled to Bury and thence to the Castle of Framlingham. Northumberland, pursuing her, halted his army at Cambridge. And for a week Cambridge, both town and University, was undecided in its loyalties. Northumberland persuaded the Vice-Chancellor Sandys to his support, but by the end of the week there had been so many desertions from his army that in despair he and Sandys walked solemnly to Market Hill and hopefully proclaimed Queen Mary. It was a little too late. Next day both were arrested, Northumberland in King's and Sandys in the Regent House, and both were conducted to London and the Tower. There they were very soon joined by Nicholas Ridley, Master of Pembroke. Cambridge, fortunately for its own peace, has not often spent a week of such breathless excitement. Incidentally, Northumberland ended not long after on the scaffold, but Sandys ultimately became Archbishop of York; which shows how chancy life for the eminent was in the sixteenth century.

So long as Mary lived neither of the Universities was likely to overlook the dangers of the times. Cambridge did not suffer from any fierce persecution, though there was a good deal of reactionary legislation. Cardinal Pole, the Chancellor, was also Chancellor of Oxford, which was his own University, and consequently he was far more interested in that place than in Cambridge, which he seems to have left entirely alone and never to have visited. But in 1555 one terrible event shook both universities: the burning at Oxford of Cranmer, Latimer, and Ridley. Though their martyrdom took place at Oxford, they were all Cambridge men and had all taught and been prominent in Cambridge for many years. At the same time the citizens of Cambridge had a glimpse themselves of the Marian flames when John Hullier of King's was burnt on Jesus Green, adjoining Midsummer Common.

The reign of Philip and Mary gave Oxford the Cambridge martyrs, but it gave Cambridge the great college of Gonville and Caius. Gonville Hall dated, as we have seen, from 1348; in 1529 there was admitted a student named Caius, whose name was probably a Latinised form of Kaye and is always pronounced " Keys." In 1533 he was elected a Fellow of Gonville and soon after proceeded to Padua to study medicine. Caius' subsequent career is remarkable; although a devout and unreformed Catholic, he was physician to Edward VI, and Elizabeth I as well as of Mary, and he became and remained till his death in 1573 the most eminent medical scientist in the country, as well as the richest. In 1557 he obtained a Patent from Philip and Mary to remodel and refound his old college, which ever since has been known officially as Gonville and Caius, and for all other purposes as Caius (" Keys ") *tout court*. It remains very largely the home of medical students, for the co-founder himself gave them special privileges. Only the holders of medical Fellowships, he laid down, might travel abroad to pursue their studies, and then preferably only to Bologna, Padua, or Paris. Theology and civil law, in the opinion of Dr. Caius, might be studied just as well in Cambridge as anywhere else.

During the reign of Mary Oxford had rather the larger share of royal patronage, due, of course, to her much closer adherence to the doctrines of the old faith. Cambridge, as a home of the reformed doctrines, came more into royal favour with the accession of Elizabeth I. Through the whole of that long reign the University prospered, partly because the queen smiled on it, but even more because the great Cecil, afterwards Lord Burghley, was its Chancellor for close on forty years. Oxford only had the Earl of Leicester as Chancellor, but since Leicester had a great flair for worldly success, this probably suited Oxford very nicely.

Cecil was a more outspoken Protestant, even Puritan, than ever the queen could show herself to be. But he was sufficiently clear-sighted to realise the potential dangers that lay in encouraging too extreme, too left-wing a form of religious thought. For forty years the history of Cambridge is primarily the history of Protestantism in England. Cecil's wise guidance of the University, though he had the whole State to guide as well, established the new religion and discouraged its extremists. Cecil also, quite early in his chancellorship, insisted on a code of other reforms, disciplinary and administrative, which pulled up sharply the more lax and easy-going of the heads of Houses. Calvinism spread rapidly through the University in the 1560's and 1570's, though King's, true to its tradition of always being rather different, remained unaffected by Geneva. Calvinism and factiousness were always inclined to go together, but Cecil's peculiar gift was that he could see beneath the merely factious or even malicious exterior and discern whatever merit or talents there might be. His somewhat severe but beautifully balanced rule was devoted entirely to the University's well-being as the centre of learning in this country. There are two other illustrious men to whom at this time Cambridge owed a great deal, and there is a poet to whom every English-speaking person owes something ; but before looking closer at these, there is the memorable visit of the queen herself to be briefly described.

The daughter of Henry VIII would not willingly miss an orgy of learning and scholarship such as would be entailed by Cambridge entertainment; and the daughter of Anne Boleyn would never, of course, refuse an opportunity of showing off, whether her own learning or her beauty or her magnificence.

The visit was made in the blazing hot August of 1564 and lasted three days. The queen approached from Grantchester and entered the town by Queens', along Queens' Lane, which then extended across what are now Webb's Court and the Back Lawn of King's, to the west door of King's Chapel. She was received by all the civic as well as University dignitaries, by the Mayor as well as by the Chancellor and Vice-Chancellor; and she was lodged royally in King's. Cecil, in attendance as Chancellor rather than as Secretary of State, was lodged in his old College of St. John's. And the Proctors from Oxford had come over, doubtless to pick up hints for use whenever the queen should deign to visit that other place; she did so, in fact, two years later.

The programme as actually carried out would probably have prostrated any lesser person than a Tudor. It was an endless round, all day and each day, of sermons and disputations to be listened to, of plays and religious services to be sat through, and of orations and addresses to be not only listened to but also replied to in Latin or Greek, on one or two occasions extempore. Each college was visited in turn, though Jesus was cut as being too far out; and the indefatigable monarch maintained a delighted and brisk flow of talk in good Ciceronian Latin with any one who had the strength to keep up with her. Probably the greater part of the court were both bored and exhausted, but Elizabeth went right through it all from beginning to end with great and apparently genuine pleasure. There were no unfortunate incidents—nobody died suddenly of the plague—and despite the great heat, the pressing crowds, the fatigue and the noise the queen's temper remained unexpectedly sweet and amiable until the cavalcade had faded from sight in a cloud of dust along the Huntingdon Road on its way to Longstanton and the palace of the Bishop of Ely.

The two great men besides Cecil to whom Cambridge owed much of her success at this time were Mathew Parker and John Whitgift, the one Master of Corpus, the other Master of Trinity, and each in turn Archbishop of Canterbury.

Parker as Master of Corpus was first and foremost an administrator; the college estates, accounts and book-keeping were put into sound order under his guidance; and as a benefactor he almost ranks as the second founder of the college. The material benefactions were very great, but his gifts to learning are almost unequalled in the University's history, for his rescuing and collecting of Saxon and early English manuscripts, which he finally bequeathed to his college, saved for posterity a world of scholarship which must otherwise have perished. At Lambeth, his career, of course, is the ecclesiastical history of England in the critical years between 1560 and 1575, but he always, with Cecil, kept a watchful eye on the university. A strong Protestant, he yet detested the noisy and troublesome Puritan party, " these irritable precisians at Cambridge " as he called them. Like Cecil he was severe and like Cecil he was just. Cambridge was mighty lucky to be guided in these years by the wisdom of the Secretary of State and the Archbishop ; her subsequent intellectual tradition was largely formed by those two men.

Whitgift, alike as Master of Trinity and as Archbishop, was much more the strong man than Parker ever was. He was personally not without sympathy with the views of Calvin, but he saw clearly that such views were impossible when it came to running a University or an Established Church. Macaulay, because he insisted on judging a sixteenth-century prelate by nineteenth-century standards, has said some very foolish things about Whitgift. Admittedly, Whitgift was rather too severe on both Catholics and Calvinists for Cecil's taste sometimes, but there is little doubt that his insistence on the doctrine and discipline of the Establishment was as good for Cambridge as it was for the Church. Otherwise the seventeenth century, with problems almost as difficult, might have seen the University suffering as badly as Oxford actually did. Whitgift was not popular either at Trinity or Lambeth, though he was highly respected and a good deal feared. But as a practical ruler in both places he was an unqualified success.

The 1570's were a critical time in English political and religious history ; and they were actually just as critical in the sublime history of English poetry. In both Cambridge proved to be one of the decisive battlefields. In the year 1569 there was entered at Pembroke as a sizar Edmund Spenser. His University years were passed largely in some degree of poverty, but they are one of the decisive periods in our poetry. Spenser fell very much under the influence of Gabriel Harvey, a cantankerous and pedantic Fellow of Pembroke who was later nominated as Master of Trinity Hall (the nomination being set aside by the Crown) and even more cantankerous.

Despite his ill-disposition and extreme pedantry, Harvey possessed great scholarship, and was the very active leader of the school which was trying to force English poetry into a rigid Latin mould. It seems to us an absurd ambition, especially when we think of anything so unfortunate as English hexameters ; but for three or four

23

years the budding genius of Spenser was guided by Harvey along those narrow lines, and he abandoned altogether for that time the use of rhyme. Had Harvey's victory been permanent, Pembroke would have been the burial-place of native poetry ; but it was not permanent. There were other influences besides Harvey's, and Spenser escaped. Rhyme survived, and the Spenserian stanza was born. Spenser did not forget his debt to his University :

> My mother, Cambridge, whom, as with a crowne,
> He doth adorn and is adorn'd of it
> With many a gentle muse and many a learned wit.[1]

Generations later Pembroke housed another poet of equal stature : Gray. But the English hexameter is probably not the most welcome gift that Pembroke could have bestowed on us.

A symptom of the rapidly increasing Puritan influence in Cambridge is the foundation in 1584 of Emmanuel College, erected by Sir Walter Mildmay on the site of the former house of the Dominicans. Mildmay, a Christ's man, was a financier, a diplomat, a politician and a courtier. But he was also quite undoubtedly a supporter in Parliament of the popular cause of Puritanism and had even come slightly into conflict with Parker. The prevailing tone of his college was from the very outset markedly Puritan. The queen did not approve. " I hear, Sir Walter," she said severely, " that you have been erecting a Puritan foundation." " Madam," he replied, " far be it from me to countenance anything contrary to your established laws, but I have set an acorn, which when it becomes an oak, God knows what will be the fruit thereof." One of the fruits, which would have surprised the queen, was the University of Harvard at Cambridge, Massachusetts, for John Harvard was entered at Emmanuel in 1627. In fact, the college contributed extensively to make New England " Emmanuel's Land," as Cotton Mather called it.

In 1591 Cambridge performed her first act of colonisation by the foundation of Trinity College, Dublin, which was, as Fuller says, " a *colonia deducta* from Cambridge and particularly from Trinity College therein . . . and this university did so Cantabrise herself that the daughter dutifully followed the judgement of the mother in the successive choice of her chancellors." And right at the end of the century, near the end of Elizabeth's reign, came the foundation of Sidney Sussex College, the last men's college to be founded in the University with the exception of Downing. Sidney was founded in 1596 by the will of Frances Sidney, Countess of Sussex, and was

---

[1] Faerie Queene, Bk. IV, xi, 34. The " He " referred to is the " Plenteous Ouse."

29   Caius : the Gate of Honour

30   Emmanuel : the 1633 Range

built on the site in Bridge Street, now Sidney Street, near the corner of Jesus Lane, previously occupied by the Friary of the Franciscans, whose endowments and even building-materials had gone into the making of Trinity fifty years before. Sidney's great claim to historic fame—and it is surely a sufficiently heavy burden of responsibility for one small college to bear—is that Oliver Cromwell was entered as a Fellow-Commoner there in 1616. His proud college described its most eminent son, in the register of admissions and written in a later hand, as *grandis ille impostor, carnifex perditissimus*—uncommonly Oxonian sentiments for a Cambridge college. Sidney still possesses a celebrated portrait-drawing of Cromwell, of which the fame is actually greater than the iconographic importance.

And so ended the sixteenth century : the century of the Cambridge Humanists, the Cambridge Reformers, the Cambridge Prayer Book of Edward VI, the Cambridge martyrs ; the century of Erasmus and Fisher, of Cheke and Ascham, of William Cecil, Parker and Whitgift, and of Edmund Spenser. The most critical and most splendid century in her history, when the University was the centre of learning and when her sons were guiding the State from Lambeth and Whitehall through its tremendous problems.

IV   Seventeenth-Century Cambridge

CAMBRIDGE GREATLY ENJOYED THE NEW REIGN THAT BEGAN on the death of Elizabeth I. The pedantically involved and scholarly mind of James I was well in tune with the University, though there were several disgruntled Fellows and scholars who complained, as disappointed men always do, that merit was never given a chance. It is perfectly true, in fact, that royal nominees frequently found their way into Fellowships and it is also apparent that the foibles of King James were loyally imitated when it came to elections to scholarships, since it was said that " Masters of colleges have no common graces, And those that scholars are must have handsome faces."

The King of Scots on his way south from Edinburgh to be enthroned King of England stayed at Hinchingbrooke, not many miles from Cambridge. His host was Sir Oliver Cromwell, whose nephew was then aged three. The shadow of that nephew may have been thrown across town and university with devastating effect forty years later, but in 1603 every one was for King James. A deputation from the heads of colleges rode to greet him with the inevitable Latin address, and the closest and most amiable relations were at once established. The royal favour was further assured by the favour of Francis Bacon, then at last becoming really eminent ; himself a Trinity man, he never forgot Cambridge, but unfortunately his many intended benefactions remained good intentions. Cambridge, like many individual people, found Lord Verulam rather unreliable.

The king's visit in March 1615 was of more than ephemeral importance, but it occasioned a good deal of anxiety. To begin with, there was no knowing how the Puritan element, especially at Emmanuel, would behave itself ; and, secondly, there was the play.

When James had visited Oxford several years before the play had been universally pronounced a failure. Then, eighteen months earlier, in 1613, Prince Charles had paid a visit to Cambridge and had complained of the intolerable dullness of the comedy at Trinity, and the Elector-Palatine, who was with him, had gone to sleep. Moreover, the play, which was the celebrated *Ignoramus*, specially written for the occasion, was timed to continue from 8 p.m. to 1 a.m.

To the relief of every one, it proved a tremendous success. It was bawdy, learned, and involved. It gave ample opportunity for a number of gay young men to strut about and over-act, which delighted the king. It was packed with insulting references to the townsmen of Cambridge, which delighted the University, and it was in Latin, which angered the town because they could not understand a word when they were told about it. The royal scholar enjoyed it so much that he came over once more from Newmarket two months later and sat through it all over again.

The result of James's great satisfaction was the continuance of uninterrupted royal favour to the University and the confirming of the town in a position of altogether secondary importance. James quite firmly refused, at the instance of the University, to raise the borough to the status of a city. The borough might, and did, petition repeatedly, but so long as the University said no, the king also said no.[1]

It was a capital time for the University and by no means too bad for the colleges. But when King James paid his last visit the omens were already not too good. To begin with, the royal presence was almost entirely withdrawn from the public gaze owing to an attack of gout ; secondly, the plague was epidemic once more ; the summer was cold and wet and the harvest failed. And the marriage of the Prince of Wales with the papist Princess Henrietta Maria was ratified in the royal apartments at Trinity. If anything were needed to rouse the ever-present Puritan desire to make trouble, that was it.

The history of Oxford during the Civil War is rather romantic and glamorous ; that of Cambridge is indescribably dreary. It was glamorous and exciting enough at the beginning of Charles I's reign, with the election of the magnificent Buckingham as Chancellor ; admittedly the Duke's majority was only three and even that unimpressive result was faked. But the Duke became Chancellor and the Puritans raged. Even more serious, Parliament raged, and raged to some effect ; from then till the Restoration Parliament was violently hostile to the University and markedly friendly to the town. The assassination of Buckingham two years later deprived

[1] Cambridge was granted the status of a city in 1951.—B.D.G.L.

the University of its most influential friend and of a great benefactor ; his gift to the Library of a priceless collection of Oriental manuscripts was not his only service, though it may have been his most lasting.

Charles, backed up by Laud at Oxford, imposed the royal authority on the University and the colleges alike, and had little difficulty in doing so. Neither Charles nor, indeed, many other people were conscious of the disapproval of a young man at Christ's called John Milton. He found almost as much to disapprove of at Cambridge as he did later in a larger world. One of his relatively few moments of good humour was occupied by writing some ponderously unfunny Humorous Verses on the Cambridge carrier Thomas Hobson, of Hobson's Choice. Hobson's Conduit and the two runnels along Trumpington Street also keep alive the name of that great and prosperous man, that seventeenth-century combination of Carter Paterson and the Green Line 'Bus.

The year 1640 must have cheered up Milton as much as it cast down the king. Oliver Cromwell was returned as M.P. for the town of Cambridge, and the town was well revenged for the insults of *Ignoramus*. Oxford in the 1640's is forever associated with Charles and Henrietta and their court. Cambridge in the 1640's is as closely associated with Cromwell, a fact which does not make for romantic narrative. The next eight years are occupied with expulsions and dispossessions, Anglican humiliations and Puritan triumphs, Parliamentary repressions, commissions, and visitations.

When civil war broke out, most of the colleges hastened to pack up their plate and send it to fill the royal treasury, but much of it was unfortunately intercepted by Cromwell, who was already virtually dictator of Cambridge and the Eastern Counties. The Puritan party in the University was much cheered and encouraged by a Parliamentary ordinance in 1643 for the Utter Demolishing of all Monuments of Superstition or Idolatry. As a result, the iconoclastic hands of one William Dowsing were laid ruthlessly on every church in Cambridge and on every college chapel. At Peterhouse Dowsing " pulled down two mightie great angells with wings." At Pembroke " we broak ten cherubims." At Queens' " we beat down about 110 superstitious pictures and broak down ten or twelve apostles' pictures in their hall." But the superb glass in the windows of King's chapel escaped ; how it escaped remains a mystery.

After the king's defeat at Naseby the townsmen began to get above themselves to an alarming extent. Already the University was impoverished and seriously disorganised by the many expulsions that had taken place among the heads of colleges, and disputes,

31   Clare, from King's Bridge

32   Christ's : the Fellows' Building

33   Emmanuel : the Gallery and Cloister

petitions and counter-petitions dragged themselves out interminably till the Restoration. Parliament took over the function of interference previously performed by the king and imposed restrictions of an intolerable severity on Fellows and undergraduates alike ; they even caused to be prohibited anything in the nature of " feasts and banquets." Even so, Cambridge was still regarded by Parliament as one of the important centres of opinion, and when the execution of the king had almost immediately been followed by that of the Chancellor of the University, Lord Holland, Cambridge, like Oxford, was required to give formal assent to the new republican government. It did so, of course ; there was no alternative but total suppression.

It is not impossible, indeed, that had the Commonwealth survived the Universities would both have been suppressed. Attacks were constantly made against them, and the chief attacker was Milton, then at his height as an unbridled political pamphleteer. His criticisms of the place where he had received his own education at almost no cost to his family were, as might have been expected, harsh and captious, but they were also unjustified and ignorant. Milton was not the only critic ; there were many others who accused the Universities of being " nurseries of wickedness " and " dens of formal droanes."

The majority of "formal droanes" at Cambridge were doubtless much relieved when Monk crossed the Tweed early in 1660 and the Restoration was seen to be imminent. Emmanuel probably did not share in this relief, and was not particularly pleased when, eighteen months later, William Sancroft was appointed Master, for the future Archbishop declared his intention at once of removing " that former singularity which rendered us heretofore so unhappily remarkable." The actual Restoration was greeted as enthusiastically in Cambridge as it was everywhere else in England, even by the townsmen. But the latter were not pleased when Charles II, in June 1660, assured the University of his determination to maintain all its former charters, privileges, and immunities.

The defeat of the Puritan ascendancy meant a newly recovered intellectual freedom for Cambridge. And the great and immediate result of this was the emergence of the Cambridge Platonists, a school of religious philosophy which may be said to represent the advanced liberal thinking of the time and a reconciliation between religion and reason, opposed to the reactionary thinking of Laud and Hobbes. The Cambridge Platonists, such as Whichcote, Cudworth and More, have had as great an influence on English thought as had their predecessors of a hundred and seventy years earlier, the Cambridge Humanists.

The home of the Cambridge Platonists, moreover, was also the home of Isaac Newton. He went up to Trinity in 1661, was elected a Fellow six years later, and divided the rest of his long life between Cambridge and London, the greater part being spent in Cambridge. If the University had contributed nothing else to the world Newton alone would justify its existence—to have produced the greatest of human intellects is almost glory enough for any University. Wordsworth, who was up at the neighbouring college, St. John's, sixty-five years after Newton's death uttered, apropos of Roubiliac's statue at Trinity, one of the two couplets which between them say all that can be said of Newton: " The marble index of a mind . . . "; the other couplet was uttered by Pope: " God said, let Newton be . . . "

It must be admitted that Cambridge made a readier submission to the republican regime than did Oxford. This is symptomatic of the difference between the two in the field of political philosophy. But the odd thing is that, despite the University's immediate Cromwellian past, Charles II showed considerable affection for " Our University of Cambridge." Perhaps this was because it was so handy for Newmarket, which he constantly visited. At any rate, he exercised to the full what may be politely called a *congé d'élire* when it came to vacancies in high University office. For example, when in 1674 the second Duke of Buckingham fell from favour, the king announced that he was now " incapable of discharging any longer the office he bore of Chancellor of our University either to our satisfaction or your benefit." And in the duke's place he warmly commended " our dearly beloved son, James Duke of Monmouth." The royal and, what was important, Protestant bastard was unanimously elected. Six years later a precisely similar letter was written, beginning " Whereas the undutifull behaviour of our Naturall Son, James Duke of Monmouth," and recommending the second Duke of Albemarle.

The reign of Charles II was really remarkable for little in Cambridge so far as the political world was concerned, while intellectually it was at one of its peaks. But there was a remarkable number of visits from royalty, surely more than at any time before or since. Newmarket again, probably. There were the Duke and Duchess of York in 1670, rather surprisingly with Barbara Castlemaine, who was presented with a " fair quarto bible." There was the Prince of Orange, the future William III, in the same year ; he was described as having a " smooth and meagre face," which must have exactly described him at the age of twenty. There was the king himself in 1671. The Duke of York's second duchess, Mary of Modena, came in 1680 with her step-daughter, the future Queen Anne, and was described as " very handsome, pretty tall, something pale-faced, and a little outlandish-like swarthy couller." And in 1681 the king and his Portuguese queen paid a visit together in tremendous state, coming over, of course, from Newmarket. The Grand Duke of Tuscany, a famous traveller with the illustrious name of Cosimo de' Medici, also paid a visit and complained that he could understand University Latin even less than English. The pronunciation must indeed have seemed peculiar to Italian ears.

Even more picturesque than a Portuguese queen or an Italian duchess or grand duke, possibly even more remarkable than Lady Castlemaine, was the Ambassador from the Emperor of Morocco, who made an official visit in 1682. This eminent Moslem, a " pretty lusty man of a very swarthy complexion," after being rendered a little indisposed by a banquet of soused eels, sturgeon, and salmon, was compelled to lie down and rest in the Lodge of the Provost of King's. He recovered in time to receive the honorary degree of M.A.

It is worth noticing that Charles, who was not perhaps deeply concerned at heart with the Established Church as opposed to the Roman, was very properly indignant at the liberty taken by parsons and students of divinity in wearing periwigs of an unbecoming length and at the " supine and slothful habit of reading their sermons." If Charles had to listen to University Sermons, he liked them delivered " by memory and without book." That way, of course, they would be shorter, with any luck.

James II afflicted Cambridge during his brief reign in the same way that he did Oxford. There were expulsions of Protestants, installations of Papists, reputed Papists, and time-serving converts not only in the colleges but in the town as well. Mayors and aldermen were removed by royal authority as easily as heads and professors.

The accession of the " meagre-faced " William III restored the Protestant *status quo* and gave a fillip to the Whig proclivities of both university and town, which the Tory Queen Anne did little to disturb.

For one thing, however, the reign of Anne is notable in Cambridge. The Professorship of Chemistry was established in 1703, the first holder of the Chair being John Vigani, who had taught chemistry in the university for twenty years previously. The consequences of that step have not been unimportant for Cambridge.

After that, however, the University settled down to its eighteenth-century privacy, unmolested by Parliament, hardly interfered with by royalty, free to pursue its academic, pluralistic, slothful, learned, quarrelsome, bibulous, self-contained and supremely self-satisfied way. The fate that overtook the Master of Magdalene in 1690 would hardly have overtaken him in, say, 1740. Being rebuked by Archbishop Sancroft for drunkenness and loose living, he did penance by four days' complete abstinence and died of it.

V Georgian Cambridge

EVERY ONE IS FAMILIAR WITH THE TRADITIONAL PICTURE OF an eighteenth-century don. Both the Cambridge and the Oxford variety have been satirised over and over again. This traditional picture shows a paunchy, bag-wigged person in a voluminous gown, drinking a great deal of port and brandy, sleeping with his bedmaker, ignoring his pupils unless they were of noble birth, in which case he toadied quite unblushingly, wanting in scholarship but active in petty intrigue.

The picture is not wholly untrue, for some Cambridge dons conformed to it in every respect. But not every don and probably not even the majority of dons. Most of them, for one thing, were too poor. The average don was neither comfortably endowed with an income nor of particularly distinguished birth.[1] His home, his whole world, was not even Cambridge, but his college ; he had no access to the social world beyond, he saw no society beyond that of his own Fellows, and if he wanted to keep his job he was condemned to celibacy. In fact, college life among the senior members must have been rather like monastic life just before the Dissolution.

From the moment when the Hanoverian dynasty was safely established and the University had suitably expressed its horror at the Scottish rebellion, Cambridge settled down to over a century of being left to itself. Royalty occasionally visited the place, on its way to or from Newmarket, to sight-see or to be given an honorary degree. The first two Georges paid one visit each, the third and fourth paid none ; royal dukes came from time to time and occasionally foreign royalty. But the relations between throne and University that had existed under the Stuarts existed no more, and have never since been recalled. Nor did Parliament bother its head about the place, as it had done in the 1650's ; that was left to the nineteenth and twentieth centuries.

[1] D. A. Winstanley, *Cambridge in the Eighteenth Century*, 1922.

At the same time, it was not really possible for Cambridge to keep entirely out of politics, for its Chancellor from 1748 to 1768 was the Duke of Newcastle, whose whole life was party politics. He applied himself to the task of being Chancellor with embarrassing thoroughness, constantly paying visits, being entertained, ordering Loyal Addresses whenever a royalty was born, married or deceased, and correcting the drafts of those addresses like a schoolmaster correcting a boy's Latin prose. The successive Vice-Chancellors enjoyed no peace whatever while Newcastle was Chancellor.

Nevertheless, despite Newcastle, it was the colleges that counted during that epoch and not the University. Trinity was Trinity, King's was King's, Pembroke was Pembroke, and the sixteen heads of colleges were sixteen independent but co-equal dictators. The Vice-Chancellor was head of his college first and Vice-Chancellor second.

As for the undergraduates, the great majority were poor, humble, obscure and, despite tutorial neglect, hard-working; mostly hoping to take orders and get a parish that would support them in something just short of penury. The small minority, a very small one, were sons of rich parents and were, as their predecessors were and their successors have often been, noisy and a source of much mouth-pursing on the part of the townsmen. Sometimes they were even apt to be a nuisance, as when they had the habit of turning respectable women upside down in Petty Cury. The puritanical East Anglian townsfolk did not find this funny, but had not yet evolved the means of getting their own back by their skill in trade. Consequently the young men won every time if their fathers were sufficiently important.

One son of a highly important father did not behave in that rumbustious manner. Horace Walpole of King's, son of the Prime Minister, Lord Orford, who had also been a Kingsman, lived an intellectual though certainly not a hard-working life, much of which was spent in talk with the shy, fastidious and scholarly Gray of Peterhouse, and formerly at Eton with Walpole. Cambridge was Gray's home for nearly the whole of his life, and, though he was probably the shyest and most retiring don in the whole place, even he suffered from the attentions of the gayer and noisier undergraduates. There was an unfortunate practical joke with a rope-ladder and a tub of cold water, which induced the indignant poet to migrate from Peterhouse and cross Trumpington Street to Pembroke. At a time when Cambridge was not rich in eminent men, he is among the most illustrious, but he took infinite pains to hide his talents under a bushel of unproductive indolence. He must be the laziest as well as the most fastidious of major poets.

Cambridge was, unquestionably, lazy. There was little reason for it to be anything else, since there were no Royal Commissions to interfere with it. But sometimes when there was serious business to be done it could apply itself with a will. There is, for example, an account of an election to the Provostship of King's in 1742, which was undertaken with some, if not all, of the solemnity customary with Cardinals in Conclave. " The Fellows went into Chapel on Monday before noon ; after prayers and sacrament they began to vote. Thus they continued, scrutinising and walking about, eating and sleeping, some of them smoaking . . . at two in the morning there was never a more diverting or more curious spectacle. Some wrapped in blankets, erect in their stalls like mummies ; others asleep on cushions, like so many Gothic tombs. Here a red cap over a wig, there a face lost in a rug. One blowing a chafing-dish with a surplice sleeve, another warming a little negus." [1] On the second day of the scrutiny a Provost was given to King's and to the world.

The conditions of life were of course very conducive to the production of remarkable characters. Even the town managed to produce one, Jacob Butler, who died aged eighty-four in 1765. He was the owner of the Stourbridge fair-ground and lord of the manor of Barnwell. Being six foot four in height, he each year invited to dinner all the dwarfs and giants who were on view at the fair.

At the beginning of this epoch the greatest and most remarkable man in Cambridge was Richard Bentley, made Master of Trinity in 1700. For the next forty years he maintained an incessant feud with the Fellows, who loathed and feared him. After ten years they tried to have him removed, but were unsuccessful ; then they persuaded the Vice-Chancellor to deprive him of his degrees, which soon had to be restored ; the war, much aggravated on both sides, continued till its climax in a magnificent battle which long raged in Trinity and in the Court of King's Bench. But nobody except the Vice Master could remove the Master of Trinity, although the Bishop of Ely had in fact exercised his legal right and had deprived him. And the Vice Master refused. So Bentley just stayed there till his death in 1742. He was dictatorial, overbearing, insolent and unconstitutional in college life, but he was the greatest classical scholar of his day, with an European reputation that still survives ; and he provided the University with an observatory and with a chemical laboratory. But though head and shoulders above every contemporary except Newton in intellectual stature, he was before everything else Master of Trinity ; he didn't care a fig for the University or the Bishop of Ely or the Court of King's Bench, but he cared

[1] Cooper, *Annals of Cambridge*, Vol. IV.

everything for his college and for his own powers as its head. He would certainly have resisted any Royal Commission with complete success.

Equally famous, and equally great as a classic, was Porson at the other end of the century; he lost his Fellowship of Trinity in 1792 owing to his refusal to take orders, and not having the battling qualities of Bentley he retired to the Temple in London. Porson was a very great scholar, a great drinker and an indefatigable writer of satiric verse. He did not think much of German scholarship and observed that " The Germans in Greek are sadly to seek." But he enjoyed the company of certain German professors, provided they were good drinkers :

> I went to Strasbourg, where I got drunk
> With that most learn'd Professor Brunck ;
> I went to Wortz, where I got more drunken
> With that more learn'd Professor Ruhnken.

There cannot have been much wrong with a period that produced Newton, Bentley and Porson and in which the undergraduates successively included Gray, Horace Walpole, Sterne, Coleridge and Wordsworth ; Orford, Halifax, Camden, Chesterfield, Pitt, Castlereagh and Wilberforce. But it has not been the habit of Cambridge to think of its *alumni* as the Archbishops or Prime Ministers which they may subsequently have become. It prefers to think of this age as that of Newton, Bentley and Porson, who were Trinity men and scholars all their lives.

Not all the heads of houses were Bentleys, though they would all have liked to be ; not every Fellow was a Newton, and it must be admitted that most of them had no such ambition. The legends and stories of eighteenth-century Cambridge do not concern themselves with the obscure and the unremarkable ; there were quite enough remarkable figures to fill volumes, as indeed they have done. Professor Ridlington of Trinity Hall is the traditional type in a remarkably pure form. When supposed to be dying of dropsy he ordered himself a whole boiled chicken and five quarts of beer. He recovered. The traditional undergraduate of the period is typified by two young men who got into trouble in 1749 for carousing at an inn till four o'clock on Sunday morning and then going to the Market Cross and " in a riotous manner eating lobsters and drinking port there." [1] The popular idea of University preferment at that time is illustrated by Richard Watson of Trinity, who began as a mathematician, was made Professor of Chemistry in 1764, when " he had never read a syllable on the subject nor seen a single experiment in

[1] Quoted by Winstanley, *op. cit.*

34   Magdalene : in the Pepysian Library

35   Trinity Hall : Wine Table in the Combination Room

37   Market Hill on a Saturday afternoon

36   Great St. Mary's from across King's Parade

t," and seven years later became Regius Professor of Divinity, having never studied theology at all until his election. It is only right that he should have ended up as Bishop of Llandaff.

Eighteenth-century Cambridge owed its character to two things: freedom from outside interference and the relative difficulty of communication with London when compared with the much better communication between London and Oxford. Until 1740 conditions were very little easier than in the days of Hobson the carrier; in 1741, for the first time, a daily post was established with London, but the first mail-coach direct to Cambridge was that from London to Wisbech, which was not established till 1792 and was timed from London to Cambridge in seven hours and a quarter. Cambridge was fortunate; the experiments of Newton, the Bentley War, the constantly pursued scholarship, the gargantuan eating and drinking, the graceful and elegant building continued as undisturbed by the outer world as the slow-moving Cam by its own almost imperceptible current.

Although only one new college was founded at this period, there were several benefactions of great importance. George I was persuaded in 1715 to buy the great library of John Moore, Bishop of Ely, and to present it to the University, having paid £6,000 for it. Then in 1719 Dr. John Addenbrooke, Fellow of St. Catharine's, bequeathed about £5,000 to found a small hospital in the town; this became "Addenbrooke's," in Trumpington Street, and is now one of the most famous hospitals in England. The year 1740 saw another handsome addition to the University Library by the bequest of the manuscript collection formed by Thomas Baker of St. John's. This sturdy Tory had been ejected from his Fellowship in 1716, through his attachment to the Jacobite cause, but continued quite undisturbed in his rooms in college till his death at the age of eighty-three.

A more important bequest was that of Sir George Downing, who died in 1749 and left his estates in trust for the ultimate founding of a college in the university. After many disputes among trustees and so on, Downing College came formally into existence in 1800. It is architecturally rather distinguished.

Equally munificent was the bequest, in 1816, of Lord Fitzwilliam, who left £100,000 and all his collections to the university for the establishing of a museum. Subsequent benefactions have made the Fitzwilliam one of the most distinguished museums and galleries in the country.

VI   Victorian and Edwardian Cambridge

THE REIGN OF VICTORIA SAW CHANGES IN THE UNIVERSITY more revolutionary than anything that had happened since the Dissolution of the Monasteries. The reforming zeal of liberals was felt here as in Oxford and at Westminster, and by the middle of the century Cambridge found itself compelled to become "useful."

But the century opened with Cambridge continuing to be its old eighteenth-century self; Byron was up at Trinity, boxing, pistol-shooting, swimming in the pool above Grantchester which still bears his name, doing little work in the academic sense, but forming close intellectual friendships as well as friendships rather less intellectual but a good deal more passionate. However, this Cambridge of the "Bucks"—of great drinking, of riotous driving of tandems through the narrow streets, of fashionable prize-fighters, of privileged noble-men undergraduates, of mail-coaches and flying-coaches and stage-coaches—was soon abolished by progress and reform.

The first warning came within five years of the Reform Bill, when an interfering M.P. for the town of Cambridge moved in the House that a Commission be appointed to enquire into the state of the University; this was defeated, but it was a pretty revenge on the part of town for its past humiliations at the hands of gown. In fact, so little did either senior or junior members of the University feel themselves in need of reforming that Lord Canterbury in 1837 presented a petition to the Lords signed by 753 resident graduates and undergraduates against any interference with the University statutes. In reply to this gesture, poor Lord Radnor could only produce a petition with 136 signatures in favour of a reform of the statutes. These statutes, incidentally, were still those laid down in the reign of Elizabeth I. Despite this triumph the University was becoming anxious for the future, and in 1844 the newly elected

38

Chancellor, Northumberland, was prayed to " uphold the honour of our University, maintain its privileges, and, if need require, defend its rights." Another motion similar to that of 1837 was defeated in the House in 1845, but a fatal piece of treachery in 1848 brought revision of the statutes perceptibly nearer. A Memorial from graduates and former members of the University was presented to the Prime Minister, the reformer Russell, begging for a Royal Commission of Enquiry on the grounds that the University was not advancing the interests of useful learning and that changes were necessary in order to increase its efficacy. That was the end. The Royal Commission was appointed in 1850, and eight years later the Statutes of Queen Elizabeth were replaced by a brand new set of modern ones. These were revised from time to time, and the result is modern Cambridge. The colleges are second to the University, the University is in the hands of the House of Commons and the Treasury. The good or ill effects of this can be discussed later, but at the time the appointment of a Commission was, quite rightly, regarded as an inexcusable infringement of rights. The one hope for the future was that the Prince Consort had been elected Chancellor in 1847. The chief agent in his election was Whewell, that Master of Trinity after whom is named the dreariest court in that or any other college. He also dignified the studies of moral and natural sciences by raising them to Tripos status.

The Prince undertook his Chancellorial duties with the earnestness that was characteristic of him, but for which the University was perhaps not quite prepared. In his very first year he produced a detailed scheme for widening the scope of studies, which had great effect and which could hardly be opposed by even the most reactionary obstructionist. Nobody seriously objected to the official recognition of subjects other than divinity, mathematics, and the classics, and it may even have been hoped that by bringing actual instruction into line with modern ideas, statutory reform might yet be avoided.

After all, there was a very sound line of defence, which was that such changes as were being urged by the Commission were not only an infringement of the University's often-confirmed rights, but were also contrary to the expressed wishes of the founders of colleges in the disposal of their bounty. " To open unreservedly to all candidates what was given and accepted in a particular manner was an unprecedented interference with the rights of property." [1] And so indeed, it was, but already in 1850 property and privileges were beginning to lose their sacred character.

[1] Quoted by Cooper, *op. cit.*, Vol. V.

Even a very modified form of socialism appeared, the Christian Socialism of Charles Kingsley. It is characteristic of the Prince Consort that his passion for education and social reform should have caused him to appoint Kingsley, then Professor of History, tutor to the Prince of Wales while that somewhat difficult youth was up at Trinity. The Prince of Wales cannot at any time of his life be described either as a Christian Socialist or as a particularly sound scholar, but he always retained a deep admiration for Kingsley. It is evident that Kingsley must have been more attractive to those who knew him personally than to those who have only read his works or followed the course of his most unfortunate and unsuccessful battle with John Henry Newman.

While Oxford was producing its sensational and much publicised Tractarian Movement, Cambridge naturally and inevitably went Evangelical and consequently was regarded by the great majority of people as " sound." If Kingsley be taken as typical of mid-Victorian Cambridge, it is not surprising that most High Churchmen regarded the place with grave mistrust. And since Evangelicalism, though popular, was hardly fashionable, it is natural that Oxford should have had the privilege of trying to educate the greater number of the more modish type of young man.

Kingsley while at Magdalene was certainly not the modish young man, though he did take boxing-lessons from a negro prize-fighter, which was rather dashing. Nor was a more serious and far more important later member of the same little college, Charles Stewart Parnell. And ten years before Kingsley appeared at Magdalene, Trinity received in 1828 one of the greatest of her *alumni*, the young Tennyson, who there met and formed his profound and passionate friendship with Arthur Hallam.

A once very celebrated figure in Evangelical circles in Cambridge was the Rev. Charles Simeon, incumbent for fifty-three years till 1836 of Holy Trinity. He had fully as great and fully as earnest a following as had Newman at Oriel, though he was undeniably a less romantic figure. It is safe to guess that Simeon was never, in the seventy-seven years of his life, anything but absolutely certain of his faith. Though he was a Kingsman, he was one of the most influential evangelical leaders of his day and helped to found the Church Missionary Society. For many years Simeon kept in the Gibbs, or Fellows', Building in King's, in the rooms with the great semi-circular window over the arch. The iron handrail which helped this evangelical veteran up the stairs still survives, and has helped to guide the participants in at least one memorable and classic party down the stairs.

39   Clare : the North Side of the Court

38   Selwyn : the Entrance Gate

40   Girton

41   Newnham

VICTORIAN AND EDWARDIAN CAMBRIDGE

Victorian Cambridge, then, presents three chief aspects which we have looked at : Evangelical and Low-Church activity ; reform of statutes, which ended the authority of the colleges ; and widening of the field of learning, on which is based her great eminence in scientific research. There is a fourth aspect, as great an innovation as the Commissioners' Statutes—the founding of the first two women's colleges. This feminine ambition for " higher education " was of course the outcome of the very desirable improvement in the women's status in the world generally.

Hostility to the women's colleges was for long almost universal at Cambridge, and might be answered by saying that Cambridge owes a great deal to the munificence of such women as Lady Clare, the Countess of Pembroke, Queen Margaret of Anjou, Lady Margaret Beaufort, and the Countess of Sussex. These pious Foundresses did, however, found their colleges for men, and their work cannot with complete appropriateness be quoted in defence of what was done at Girton and Newnham, or as a precedent for the third women's college which is now (1954) about to start work.

The women's colleges were not at the beginning officially a part of the University, but in 1947 their members were admitted to full membership of the University as a whole, and their status is now virtually equivalent to that of the men's colleges. Girton, originally established at Hitchin in 1869, was moved in another four years to its somewhat remote position on the road to Huntingdon. Newnham, whose eventual site is considerably less remote than that of Girton, was first established in 1871 when Miss Anne Clough started with five students in a house which had been rented in the town of Cambridge itself. In 1872 she moved to Merton Hall, and in 1875 to Newnham. Her successor as Principal, in 1892, was Mrs. Henry Sidgwick, whose husband, the famous philosopher who had been largely responsible for the founding of Newnham, lived in the college during his wife's period as Principal.

In 1882 there was founded a men's college, Selwyn, with the particular aim of providing a University education, combined with strict economy and simple living, for practising members of the Church of England. Queen Victoria gave it a Charter exactly on the lines of that granted to Keble College, Oxford. The advent of Selwyn was greeted with displeasure by Cambridge liberals, flushed with their victory in the Universities Religious Tests Act, who saw the flank of their position turned by means of a new foundation. One of the most formidable opponents of the new college was Oscar Browning.

Oscar Browning was, to all intents and purposes, King's between

6* 41

1875 and 1908. He embodied most of the characteristics that tended to make some other Kingsmen unpopular with the rest of the University : a sound conviction that they are quite unlike other men ; an intellectual intolerance of those outside the college and a tolerance of almost everything inside it ; a closer relationship between dons and undergraduates than exists elsewhere ; an attitude of pronounced liberalism in politics, religion, and morals ; and a very healthy contempt for the cult of athletics, though the traditionally tolerant Kingsman has never objected to their practice. About twenty years ago the King's boat contrived to make four bumps on the four successive nights of the May Races. This surprising performance was the signal for a flood of angry letters and telegrams from former Kingsmen all over the country, mostly elderly parsons, protesting at this dangerous and deplorable intrusion of the competitive athletic spirit. Oscar Browning fully shared, while he was at Cambridge, the true Kingsman's attributes, and hated athleticism while liking and supporting athletics. He once crossed the Alps on a tricycle.

This much-loved and widely disliked " O. B." left Cambridge in 1908, having gone up to King's in 1856. He died in 1923, and is therefore a link between the crowded, active, scientific, Government-aided University of to-day and the University of the days before Commissions, reform, widenings and openings-up, when the railway was new and much discouraged, when King's was limited to a few celibate Fellows and a handful of scholars all of whom must be Etonians, when St. John's was still without its Gilbert Scott chapel, and when elderly members of Trinity high-table could still remember the drinking achievements of old Porson and the odd behaviour of young Lord Byron.

One of Cambridge's achievements during this period was the building-up of the Fitzwilliam Museum into the European institution that it now is : a great collection in a very great building and beautifully arranged. Lord Fitzwilliam bequeathed, together with £100,000, an important Rembrandt, a Titian and a Palma Vecchio amongst other things, and throughout the nineteenth century bequests of Dutch and Flemish paintings, following the nineteenth century collectors' fashion, poured in. The Fitzwilliam shares with Dulwich the distinction of being an important point of study for the less-known eighteenth-century English painters ; it is beaten by the Ashmolean in the matter of Old Master drawings, but it is very rich in English drawings. It also possesses a highly important collection of majolica, which is fine for those who like majolica. Among its benefactors, the Fitzwilliam counts the name of Courtauld as of equal importance with that of its founder, and it has good reason for doing so.

Nineteenth-century Cambridge developed with great ease into Edwardian Cambridge. It soon got over its shocks from constitutional revolution, accepted readily enough (in due course) its expanded field of study, took for granted its archæological crimes and architectural experiments, and settled down to a new life,[1] in the years that used to be called " pre-War."

Important years, when the Cavendish Laboratory was building up its present illustrious reputation ; when the Musical Society was astonishing musical Europe by its courageous enterprise ; when Rupert Brooke at King's was to some the most important young man of his year, and when to others his less articulate brother Alfred was even more important ; when the Marlowe Dramatic Society was discovering long-forgotten Elizabethan treasures ; when horse-trams existed and the Union Debates were taken more seriously than a few years later. The distant humiliations of the Boer War were forgotten, which was relatively easy, since Cecil Rhodes had not revenged himself on Cambridge as he had on Oxford.

When the First, or Great, German War broke out Cambridge, as a University, went into eclipse. When the war ended, life began again, but it was not easy to re-establish contact between 1913 and 1919. Some much-loved and fanciful individuals like Mansfield Forbes of Clare, Theo Bartholomew of Peterhouse and Charles Sayle of Trumpington Street were among those who preserved some kind of liaison. But Cambridge of the very early twenties was an odd place. For the first year or two after 1919 there was some relaxation of academic standards ; Pass-degrees were permitted where before only Honours were aimed at ; a rather large number of undergraduates were idle, in that they spent too much of their time in dancing and in using up the stocks of 1911 hocks and champagnes that still survived in some of the college cellars. Such relaxation of standards was but temporary, and the traditional high level was very soon insisted upon. But it does appear that the post-war undergraduate of 1919 was less burdened with a sense of prematurely-adult responsibility than the post-war undergraduate of 1945. Nevertheless, the continuity of the essential Cambridge was not broken by the 1914–18 War. It was, indeed, symbolised in a Royal way. Pre-war Oxford had been honoured by the presence at Magdalen of the Prince of Wales, but after the war Cambridge was honoured by the presence at Trinity of the Princes Albert and Henry.[2] Since their grandfather

---

[1] Well described by Charles Tennyson : *Cambridge from Within*, 1913.
[2] Later H.M. King George VI and H.R.H. the Duke of Gloucester.

Edward VII and their uncle the Duke of Clarence had also been at Trinity, and their great-grandfather the Consort had been Chancellor of the University, this affirmation of continuity in a tradition came at the right time.

VII Mediæval Cambridge

THE TOURIST IN SEARCH OF THE ANTIQUE IN CAMBRIDGE IF, like the majority of tourists, he be equipped with more enthusiasm than discrimination must always be careful. There are several traps into which the careless visitor is liable to fall. He probably will have got beyond the stage of mistaking revivalist Gothic for real fourteenth century, but he is likely to be still in the stage of confusing them critically. He tends to the admiration of an old bit of wall because it dates from 1386 and to the disparagement of a new chapel or hall because it dates from 1836. The former is rare, and therefore interesting, but mere antiquity does not necessarily make it beautiful nor always even picturesque. The latter is " imitation Gothic," but that does not necessarily make it contemptible nor always even comic.

There is plenty of every period from the fourteenth to the twentieth centuries—quite enough of everything to do away with the red-herring of rarity value. When the tourist is in search of the really ancient he must not confuse it, when he finds it, with architecture. And when he is in search of architecture he must at least make the attempt to judge it as the expression of whatever age it belongs to. In a place like Cambridge, where examples of every period jostle each other, it is not wise to look at any particular building simply in relation to its neighbours, as one would do in a homogeneous place like Bath or the Edinburgh New Town. It must be looked at also in relation to other buildings of the same period and in the same idiom. It is desirable to go through both these processes if the tourist wants to get the most out of his tour. He should also remember that he is in a town whose history is unlike that of any other town in England with the exception of Oxford ; in which building for six centuries has been almost exclusively an affair of college-chambers, halls, chapels and libraries and was never seriously, until the early nineteenth century, an affair of domestic architecture.

In college after college he will see the same basic arrangement : a court or courts (which at Oxford are called quads), a dining hall, a library which is sometimes a separate building and sometimes part of something else, a chapel, and ranges of buildings in which live the dons and undergraduates. The outsides of these ranges are naturally dictated by their internal arrangement, which at both Universities is an essential characteristic ; rooms are not (in all but the most modern blocks) arranged in corridors, but in staircases with two sets on each floor, so that one's neighbours are not in the rooms next door, but in the rooms opposite. This staircase unit means that the front of each range of buildings is pierced by entrances at frequent and regular intervals. The women's colleges are arranged with the rooms opening off corridors, which is easy enough with bed-sitting rooms.

The general lay-out of Cambridge has undergone four main modifications since Saxon times, of which two have occurred since 1800. The first is the shifting of the centre of gravity from the original settlement of Grantebrigge across the river to the town which clustered round the churches of St. Benet [1] or St. Botolph, and the consequent growth of Trumpington Street–King's Parade–Trinity Street, and of Milne Street running roughly parallel to it and nearer to the river. The second is the sweeping away of Milne Street by Henry VI, and the consequent disappearance of the hythes, or wharves, which opened off it on to the river for the ships coming up from King's Lynn. Milne Street had been till then the busiest street of the town ; with its disappearance the river above the Great Bridge became a tranquil stream, undisturbed except for a very few barges. The third modification was the early nineteenth-century growth of a residential Cambridge, mainly round Parker's Piece to the east and south-east. The fourth is the growth, within the last forty years, of another and highly refined residential district across the Backs to the west, chiefly between the Madingley and Barton roads ; here live many of the married dons in very earnest and cultured comfort.

Mediæval Cambridge had three main streets ; Bridge Street, now represented by Bridge Street and Sidney Street, Regent Street and with St. Andrew's Street prolonging its original course ; High Street, now represented by St. John's Street, Trinity Street, King's Parade,

[1] For the Saxon origin of this part of Cambridge one recalls F. W. Maitland's famous sentence : " The tower of St. Benet's church raises its protest." See his *Township and Borough*, p. 99.—B.D.G.L.

and Trumpington Street; and the vanished Milne Street. The market-place was and still is the centre of the town; in the Middle Ages it was a narrow, L-shaped affair and so remained till about 1850, when there was still a cluster of shops and houses crowding right up to the walls of Great St. Mary's.

Going back again to the Middle Ages, the tourist may, if he wishes, cross the bridge to the north-west and walk up Castle Hill. If he does he will almost certainly fall into one of Cambridge's antiquarian practical-jokes. There is a variety of earthworks to be seen, attributed by rival archæologists to Roman, Saxon or Danish authorship, and the practical-joke is that the amateur archæologist will be thrown into additional confusion by the remains of Cromwell's earthworks. Nothing is left of the masonry of the Castle. It is rather fancifully shown in Richard Lyne's pictorial map, of 1575, when some still existed.

All this north-west quarter was Cambridge at the date of Domesday, and there was comparatively little else; it was once known as the Borough and its inhabitants as " Borough-Boys." Northampton Street, near the corner of Castle Hill had, until recently, an inn called " The Borough Boy " and still has several highly picturesque and insanitary looking houses of great antiquity. On the right-hand side of Castle Hill going down is the diminutive Norman Church of St. Peter's. It is said to be the smallest Church in Cambridge, which perhaps it is, being about thirty feet long. The Victorian St. Giles' church retains from its predecessor a Norman arch and one of about 1180.

There is also nearby, where Northampton Street merges into the Backs, the oddly named School of Pythagoras or Pythagoras House. It was never a school.[1] It was originally a Norman manor-house, bought about 1270 by Walter de Merton, and the property still belongs to Merton College, Oxford. Fragments of the existing house are Norman, in a patched and altered way.

Mediaeval Cambridge east of the Cam is scattered over the whole length of the city and out on its eastern side. The best way to see it is to ignore chronology and work topographically, beginning with Bridge Street, going out past Jesus to Barnwell, and ending with Peterhouse.

In Bridge Street is St. Clement's church, originating about 1200 and with its present tower of the 1820's. The lover of early mediaeval architecture will be disappointed at seeing a great deal of fifteenth-century work, but can console himself by the reflection that otherwise the church, since the nave arches had begun to settle rather

---

[1] But Miss Clough had her students there from 1872 to 1875.

badly, would probably have fallen down. Farther east, opposite the end of St. John's Street and next to the Union, is Holy Sepulchre, which dates from about 1130. This church is always being described as one of the five round churches in England ; it would be rather more accurate to describe it as one of the five mediæval churches with a circular nave. It has been repeatedly restored, even before the Cambridge Camden Society undertook the task in 1841. It was probably impressive till its first remodelling in the fifteenth century, but now its original character is rather impaired.

A little way past the Round Church is Jesus Lane. This leads us past Jesus College, and so along Maid's Causeway to Barnwell and the Newmarket Road. In Barnwell are two important relics of the Priory. One of them is a part of the domestic buildings and was the " cellarer's checker," or receiving point for provisions coming in from outside. Close to it, a fine old house, with a Dutch gable which bears the date 1672, incorporates many fragments of the Priory stonework. Then on the main road one has the unaisled church of St. Andrew the Less. This was the gate-chapel, or *capella ad portas*, of the Priory. It is a delightful piece of Early English work, with three particularly beautiful lancet windows in its eastern wall, their decoration taking the form of deep mouldings and dark shafts of Purbeck marble.

Further out, and just beyond the railway bridge, is the excellent little Norman chapel which was once that of the Sturbridge Leper Hospital. Of twelfth-century date, it was long desecrated and in part used as a store, partly as a cottage. Now, however, it is again used for worship and its doorways, windows, chancel arch, and traces of vaulting in the chancel all have good late Norman decoration. The mere fact that it was the chapel of a Leper Hospital makes it of great historic interest.

Turning at a right angle opposite the Round Church, the mediævalist will walk down St. John's–Trinity Street till he is opposite Caius. Here on his left he will find the Church of St. Michael, which was used by the students of the extinct Michaelhouse as their chapel, and certainly was in existence around 1250. It was rebuilt by Hervey de Stanton, Chancellor of the Exchequer and a Canon of York, who was buried here in 1327. As is usual with Cambridge churches, it has been much altered, and a fire in 1849 gave Gilbert Scott his opportunity. The church, however, is very well worth visiting ; the mediæval choir stalls are interesting, the Victorian modified box-pews are far from offensive, and the roof and arches of the choir are elaborately decorated in the William Morris manner which, at any rate in the roof, is very successful. There are

42 King's : Buttresses of the Chapel

43   Old Houses opposite Magdalene

44   Old Houses in Northampton Street

redecorated sedilia of Hervey de Stanton's time, a squint (or loop-hole window) from the vestry giving on to the altar-steps, and a rather deplorable portrait of Charles I in ecstasy, said to have been presented in 1660 and showing only too evident signs of having been restored in 1881.

Opposite this church is Caius and behind Caius is Clare. Both these are fourteenth-century foundations, but both have been so extensively rebuilt—Clare at least in a civilised manner—that it is more suitable to discuss them later.

Trinity Hall, however, next door to Clare, founded also in the fourteenth century, does retain much of its original fabric, and a fair amount of it is visible now. The first court conceals beneath an elegant ashlar coating its original fabric. The mediævalist can still see the fourteenth-century work on the outside of the north range of the court, which is the side towards Trinity. The inside of the court, with its pleasant sash-windows and correct classic facing, is the work of Cambridge's most distinguished amateur architect, Sir James Burrough, Master of Caius from 1754 to 1764. His work at Trinity Hall was done between 1730 and 1745, and the hall, or west side of the court, with its elegant lantern, is remarkably satisfactory. The North side of the court was very well restored about 1929, and during the process a tiny little window of the fourteenth century was discovered in the corner where the north and west ranges meet. This relic has been thought so interesting that a gap in the otherwise intact classical facing has been made for its display.

Beyond this court is the library, a small Elizabethan building of very pleasing dull-red brick, with a crow-stepped gable. It has great charm from the outside and is interesting as being the only college library to preserve its mediæval appearance, for though it is of 1590, it has lectern stalls of the mediæval type. Just beyond the library, to the west, is a range of 1892 in " Elizabethan " bright-red brick. To see how thoroughly muddle-headed it is, it should be compared with the second court of St. John's. There is considerable relief walking back through Burrough's admirable little classic first court.

Pursuing the track of mediæval survivals, the next thing to do is to walk up into King's Parade, dive down St. Edward's Passage opposite King's Chapel and visit the Church of St. Edward. This church is so hemmed in by buildings on so cramped a site that the size of its interior is rather surprising. It was originally built about 1200, and the lower portion of the tower dates from that time. What is more important is that the present nave is very late four-teenth-century at its most light and graceful. About fifty years later, Henry VI founded King's, which entailed demolishing another church, St. John Zachary, which stood on his site. This church was used by both Clare and Trinity Hall, so the king found it necessary to obtain from Barnwell Priory the gift of the living and then to demolish the church. He achieved this in November 1446. By way of compensation, the Church of St. Edward was enlarged by a south chancel aisle for Clare and a north chancel aisle for the Hall; all three of the colleges concerned in these very royal transactions still retain their connection with the church; King's still uses the parish registers (though not very often those for marriage or birth), and many Fellows of all three are buried or commemorated there, including two Clare men who were among the translators of the Authorised Version.

Latimer preached in this church; so did Thomas Bilney, so did Thomas Barnes, members with Tyndale and Coverdale of that White Horse set which launched the Reformation on to England. From the congregation which sat here and listened to Latimer were chosen Wolsey's recruits to his Oxford foundation of Christchurch (or Cardinal College). The pulpit from which Latimer preached was removed in 1848, when the church was restored, but is now again in the church, as it has been lent by King's. St. Edward's experienced a new distinction in 1871–72 when the chaplain was Frederick Denison Maurice, Professor of Moral Philosophy, who twenty years earlier had got into trouble for his heterodoxy.

A little farther south along King's Parade is Benet Street, and a short way up Benet Street on the right is St. Benet's Church. This is the oldest church in Cambridge, and indeed in the county, with a Saxon tower of about 1050 built as the principal feature of a parish church in the town which grew up side by side with the settlement of older origin which lay north-west of it across the river. The tower still has its original timeless appearance and its sturdy peasant quality, which is repeated inside by the round-headed arch at the west end of the nave, under the tower. The little grass plot to the south of the church between the church and Corpus Old Court, with its flowers under ancient boundary walls, must be very much what William Morris meant when he talked of a *garth*.

Between Benet Street and Botolph Lane, facing on to King's Parade, is Corpus Christi College, or Corpus. The college of Elizabeth I's Archbishop Parker and the recipient of his great library, it now retains as its chief architectural distinction the Old Court, dating from 1350–60 and, despite its quite recent coating of neat rough-cast, surviving in its original form. It is the oldest complete court in Cambridge, yet the Saxon tower of St. Benet which rises above it was 300 years old before the court was begun.

For generations this court was the entire college, with its entrance not on to King's Parade but round the corner in Benet Street. The site of this entrance is still marked by a small rusticated classical archway of 1757 in the corner of the garth behind St. Benet's Church. At different times in the eighteenth century various schemes were proposed to build a new court giving a main entrance on to King's Parade; of these by far the most important was that submitted in 1773 by James Essex, a correct and admirable architect whom we shall encounter in several other colleges. His scheme was for an open three-sided court, south of the old court, where in fact the present first court is, in the classical taste and obviously designed in relation to the open court of St. Catharine's immediately opposite ; this would have been a really notable addition to Cambridge architecture, but unfortunately it was not carried out.

Nothing was carried out for another fifty years, but at last William Wilkins was charged with the task in 1822–3. Wilkins and Essex are two of the most conspicuous architects in Cambridge ; Essex remained mainly classical, while Wilkins began in the classical taste, as we shall see at Downing, and settled before long into the Gothic, as we shall see at King's. He was also, it is as well to remember, the architect of the very classical University College, London, and the very Gothic Dalmeny House in Scotland. Here at Corpus Wilkins has already become Gothic, though the long frontage on Trumpington Street is really a building of classical proportions in a Gothic dress ; in other words, despite its turrets, hood-moulds and battlements it is essentially classical architecture. The west front of the chapel, facing the main entrance, is faintly reminiscent of King's Chapel on a diminutive scale, and this impression is whimsically repeated inside by four rather inferior windows of the same early sixteenth-century Flemish type as the King's windows, on the scale relatively that a card-table is to a lawn-tennis court. Wilkins at this time either was at work on or had already completed the Hall at King's, quite one of his most successful interiors, and the Library at Corpus contains more than a hint of that hall. Here is housed Archbishop Parker's magnificent library, with its famous collection of manuscripts.

Corpus occupies the site between the two ancient little churches of St. Benet and St. Botolph. The latter may not share St. Benet's distinction of being pre-Conquest, but it certainly existed in 1190. Nothing survives of this period, and in fact the earliest part of the church is the nave, early fourteenth century, and its most attractive feature is the very lofty, narrow-pointed arch at the west end of the nave. The fanciful and elaborate font is a very Jacobean conceit, though it may be early Carolean, and in the chapel on the south side there is an elaborate monument of 1609 to Thomas Play-fair, Lady Margaret Professor of Divinity. Both the monument and its portrait-bust are covered with thick, mud-coloured paint which is peeling off ; the effect is not pretty.

Pembroke, which is the next college along Trumpington Street on the left, has not on the whole had a fortunate architectural history. Though the third oldest of the surviving colleges it not only retains nothing of its older buildings but has the most extensive display of Waterhouse's architecture in Cambridge, more even than Caius. The north and west sides of the first, or old, court are in substance more or less original, but they have been so much and so often altered that this has to be taken on trust.

Most of the original buildings were still in existence till the 1870's, though they were largely in a ruinous condition. Pembroke was the first college to possess a chapel of its own and this, built soon after 1366, continued in use till the new chapel was consecrated in 1664. It was subsequently reconstructed and turned into the library, which it still is ; it has a very fine, characteristic plaster ceiling dated 1690.

The college was enlarged in the seventeenth century by the addition of a three-sided court beyond, and to the east of, the original court. Part of this, though a little dull, is important architecturally as being the only considerable Cambridge building erected during the Commonwealth.

However, Pembroke's greatest possession is its Wren chapel. Christopher Wren's uncle, the Bishop of Ely, had been a Fellow of Pembroke some years earlier, before becoming Master of Peterhouse. We shall see how in 1628–32 he had been responsible for building Peterhouse chapel. On the outbreak of the Civil War the bishop, as he was by then, was naturally regarded in an unfavourable light by the Puritans of East Anglia and was confined in the Tower, where he spent the next eighteen years. During his imprisonment he made a vow that if ever he should be released and restored to his see and his paternal estates he would express his thanks to Almighty God by the erection of a chapel at Pembroke " for the Ornament of the University and in grateful Remembrance of his first Education, which was in that Place received." [1] In 1659, after the death of the Protector and on the eve of the Restoration, Dr. Wren was released and in 1663 he set about redeeming his vow. It was not unnatural that he should have given the commission for the new chapel to his clever young nephew, Christopher. The nephew, as an untried architect, was fortunate in his influential uncle, but the uncle and the college were supremely fortunate in their architect.

[1] Wren, *Parentalia.*

45   Holy Sepulchre

46   Holy Sepulchre : the Interior, before the Restoration of 1841
(from Ackermann's *Cambridge*)

46. Trinity Hall: the West Side of the Court

It is Wren's earliest work, four years earlier than Oxford's Sheldonian, and, if its outside proportions are not quite as perfect as might be expected even of the youthful Wren, it is nevertheless a very pleasing addition to Trumpington Street. Inside it is entirely satisfying and shows that Wren was a master from the moment he began ; the sanctuary is a sympathetic addition by the younger George Gilbert Scott. The altar-piece is attributed to Baroccio and once belonged to Sir Joshua Reynolds ; many passages in his " Discourses " must have been written round it, and it reflects a passing taste and a former standard of judgement as completely as the chapel itself reflects a permanent and lasting canon.

The rebuilding of the college became necessary during the eighteenth century and was first seriously contemplated in 1776, when a Building Fund was established in memory of the poet Gray. Had the building been actually carried out then it might indeed have been a fitting memorial to one so fastidious and sure in his tastes. As it turned out, little was done till 1871, when Waterhouse took the matter drastically in hand. The result is a quite fantastic travesty of everything Gray would have meant by architecture, and we need not, even if we could, dwell on it further. Even the college itself had qualms about what was being done under their noses when the eminent architect pronounced the old hall to be dangerously insecure and then had to demolish it with gunpowder since all other means had failed. It was suggested at the time that the college might be rechristened as well as rebuilt, and become Waterhouse to balance Peterhouse across the street.

Peterhouse, the first and also the oldest surviving college in Cambridge, possesses several endearing features as well as some interesting survivals. Its front towards Trumpington Street is not very striking, but it has no need to be : here is the beginning of the collegiate system, very nearly the beginning of the University itself, more than 650 years' continuous, unbroken tradition of habitation by dons and undergraduates, generation after generation for the whole of that period dining in the same hall, from 1286 till to-day.

The hall is the oldest surviving part of the college, and the oldest surviving collegiate building in Cambridge ; it was built immediately after the death of the founder, Hugh de Balsham, in 1286, but though it has not been rebuilt it has been much altered. The main court, substantially in its original form, was partly refaced by Sir James Burrough in the 1750's, very successfully in his usual simple, unidiomatic classic, and is rather reminiscent of his admirable work at Caius. Two doorways at either end of the screens passage by the hall are original survivals, and the antiquarian tourist may take comfort from them in gazing at the earliest examples of collegiate architecture in Cambridge. He can repeat the experience by looking at the garden front of the south side of the court and, with much more difficulty, at a battered bit of the outside wall of the kitchen.

Antiquarian value apart, Peterhouse contains three very good things of three different periods : the 1630 chapel, the 1740 Fellows' Building and the hall in its present 1870 form.

The chapel is an enchanting piece of Charles I " Gothic Survival," that rather rare style which is more readily associated with Laudian Oxford than with Puritan Cambridge. It was built in 1628-32 during the Mastership of Dr. Matthew Wren, whom we have encountered at Pembroke, and its mixture of Gothic, Renaissance and Classic elements is no doubt very shocking but is undeniably extremely attractive. The west front has two melodious little Gothic niches, which are the prettiest things imaginable, and the east window contains its original magnificent glass of an intense and remarkable blue. It is a Rubens design, and was put up at the expense of the Parliamentarian Luke Skippon, of all people, the brother of Cromwell's general Philip Skippon. It must have put the iconoclast Dowsing in a pretty quandary.

The Fellows' Building, on the north side of the first court, with its end to the street, is again by Sir James Burrough, of 1738-42. It is, of course, rigidly classical, so correct as to merit the approval of the sternest eighteenth-century critics ; it makes no concession in the smallest details to the picturesque, and is almost a reproof to the gay little chapel beside it. The poet Gray was one of its original occupants till his angry migration in 1754, and may well have regretted leaving this classical excellence for the higgledy-piggledy old-worldliness of Pembroke.

The block facing the Fellows' Building, on the south side of the first court, is the late Elizabethan library of 1590-95. It is, in contrast with the rest of the college, wholly of brick and was extended in 1633, which date is inscribed on the romantical gable-end facing the street.

Another and admirable piece of brick-building is the Master's Lodge, which stands across the street opposite the first court. This was built in 1701, and has the beautiful manners of Queen Anne domestic architecture. The new building next door to it was built, certainly and quite successfully with an eye to its neighbour, in 1926. It is very genteel and a trifle arch, and much more self-conscious about its manners.

The hall is on the south side of the main court. Although substantially its original self, it was thoroughly restored by Gilbert

Scott in 1868–71, at the moment when his rival Waterhouse was so disastrously busy across the way. It is an extremely successful piece of Victorian Gothic, and quite one of Scott's best interiors, the roof and oriel being especially good. The admirable and justly famous glass is by William Morris from designs by Burne Jones.

The passage between hall and buttery opens on to the garden, just by the fragment of ancient kitchen-wall, and across the garden is the sixteenth-century wall that separates it from the common-land known as Coe Fen. This wall is impressive and looks very solid and massive, but when some of it fell down not long ago it was found to be merely a shell inadequately filled with rubbish. Some Tudor contractor must have made a deal of money. When this wall was built, and indeed into the nineteenth century, the undrained Fen came right up to it. This part of the river and the watery meadows stretching to the Backs road still strongly suggest barely reclaimed fen-country.

The adjacent church, St. Mary the Less, was used by Peterhouse until the college built its own chapel. The first church on the site was built in the twelfth century and was dedicated to St. Peter as, in due course, was Hugh de Balsham's College. The present church with its new dedication was completed by 1352, and has not been greatly altered since. The east window is remarkable in having not only extremely beautiful decorated tracery but also modern glass of about 1890 by C. E. Kempe, which is really good and is well worth looking at. The church also boasts a well-known mural tablet to the Rev. Godfrey Washington, vicar from 1705 to 1729, with the " stars and stripes " [1] which is the rather unheraldic description of the Washington family arms. Most American visitors to Cambridge are very properly carried along to see this.

[1] Heraldically speaking : barry of four gules and argent in chief three mullets gules.

VIII   Renaissance Cambridge

THE PREVIOUS TOUR LED US, CHRONOLOGICALLY SPEAKING backwards from Trinity Hall in 1350 to Peterhouse in 1286. The second journey can combine chronological correctness with topographical convenience, and take us from King's to its immediate neighbours Queens' and St. Catharine's, out to Jesus and back by Christ's to St. John's. This covers the period from Henry VI to the beginning of the Reformation.

Peterhouse was founded in 1284, Clare (as University Hall) in 1326, Pembroke in 1347, Gonville in 1348, Trinity Hall in 1350, Corpus in 1352 ; six surviving colleges[1] in less than a century. But ninety years elapsed before the next college, King's, appeared, of which the foundation marks the great period of late Gothic or early Renaissance building in Cambridge ; architecturally it was still Gothic, but intellectually it is already Renaissance : the New Learning was beginning.

The Founder of King's himself, Henry VI, designed his great college as an institution to combat the growing modernist tendency of Lollardish free thinking, but what with the Wars of the Roses and one thing and another the royal plan for the college dwindled into a gigantic, disproportionate chapel and a moderate sized court on its north side. And thus, in fact, the college remained from its founding in 1441 till the building of the Gibbs range in 1724–31. Yet the present site of the college, as it is, was the property of the college from its foundation. The whole area south of the chapel lay reserved but fallow for centuries. The college complained to its founder that the allotted area was inadequate, but it was nearly 400 years before it occupied buildings anything like adequate to the proportions of its chapel.

King's Chapel has been written about and photographed more than any other building in Cambridge. It has been called, and indeed is, the finest flower of late Gothic in Europe. It is one of England's

---

[1] Or eight including the now defunct King's Hall and Michaelhouse.

48　Corpus Christi : the First Court

49　Corpus Christi : the Library

50 King's Chapel : the Choir Stalls

most precious possessions. Its roof is among the few complete and perfect examples of fan-vaulting on a large scale in existence, it shares with York Minster the distinction of being the only major mediæval church in England that retains intact its original windows. At every season, by every light and in every mood, the chapel is " sublime " ; it makes even the most carefully reasoned criticism seem querulous and pert, and goes on calmly and serenely reducing generation after generation to helpless surrender in face of its overwhelming beauty.

Its architectural history is fairly straightforward and well documented, though it is not altogether as the king intended it to be, and the college as a whole is even less so. Henry, in his will drawn up in 1448, lays down the main lines and proportions of the chapel and provides for a court to its south and a cloister-court to the west, neither of which was built. The actual building was slow ; in 1455 the college's white limestone quarry gave out and the works stopped for a time, when the east end had risen to about two-thirds of its full height and the west end to barely eight feet. Very little was done for the next twenty-five years, but between 1476 and 1483 quite good progress was made, which was greatly speeded up by Richard III. That Yorkist King showed tremendous energy in carrying on the work of his Lancastrian predecessor, even ordering the surveyor to imprison any one who delayed the operations. It was at this time decided to complete the choir, to glaze the choir-windows with plain glass and to roof it with timber. At the time of Richard's death in battle in 1485 this had been done and the western end of the roofed portion closed up. Thus the five easterly bays were available for use, but the seven westerly ones were not only roofless but little more than a shell perhaps ten feet high.

So the unfinished chapel remained for another twenty years, till in 1506 Henry VII and Lady Margaret, his mother, attended a service in the roofed part. Henry's very equivocal position made him cling with exceptional piety to the memory of his saintly and Lancastrian cousin, the founder. In 1508-9, during the last months of his life, this visit of two years earlier bore splendid fruit in the form of gifts for the completion of the chapel and directions to his executors to pay out similar sums for the same purpose when required. Work began immediately : the western bays were completed first ; then in 1512 the tremendous vault of the roof was begun ; then the west door, and finally the four corner towers. The stonework of the chapel as it stands was completed by 1515. Henry VI would have strongly condemned the ubiquitous display of heraldic carving in the ante-chapel. These Tudor crowned roses and portcullises, these rampant supporting beasts, do not at all conform with the founder's injunctions for " settyng aparte superfluyte of too grete curyous werkes of entaylle and besy moldyng," but they do glorify the Houses of Beaufort and Tudor and show a most devoted sense of responsibility on the part of Henry VII's executors.

This heraldic carving pleases the lover of intricacy by its extraordinary delicacy of detail, but it has the far greater merit of being on the noble scale of the building itself, a perfect harmony between architecture and sculpture.

The next undertaking was to fill the windows with stained glass worthy of the chapel. This was begun in 1515 by Barnard Flower, the king's glazier, using the glass in Henry VII's chapel at Westminster as his model. He died in 1525, and two years later, in 18 Henry VIII, an indenture [1] was drawn up between Provost Hacomblen and the glaziers Galyon Hoone of Southwark, Richard Bownde of St. Clement Danes, Reeve of St. Sepulchre, and Symonds of St. Margaret's Westminster, in accordance with which all the windows were completed except the great west one, which is nineteenth century and stands up to its illustrious neighbours on the whole pretty well. The windows are late and Flemish-seeming, and perhaps debased when compared with the best at York ; but their emotional and evocative power is unparalleled, unless it be by the roof floating above them.

The screen which divides the choir from the ante-chapel can be accurately dated to 1533–35 by the arms and cypher of Queen Anne Boleyn, which appear with those of Henry VIII. It is structurally an integral and essential part of the whole building, providing at just the right moment that transverse emphasis without which the chapel would appear intolerably long and narrow. Intrinsically it is a museum-piece of the greatest rarity, unique in England and nearly so north of the Alps. It is mercilessly intricate in detail. Admiration of it depends on whether one happens to like Italian Renaissance carving.

The organ-case above the screen is James II, and has the right mixture of richness and simplicity that one expects of the 1680's. On top of the lectern in the choir is a quite charming little figure of Henry VI, which with the lectern itself is the gift of Provost Hacomblen, who reigned over the college from 1509 to 1528.

The college in his day, and until 1723, consisted solely of a modest

---

[1] Quoted by George Vertue in his Note-book for 1731–36, where he also quotes indentures of 4 Henry VIII for the great vault, the north and south porches, the battlements and finials.

court to the north of the chapel, with its entrance on to Milne Street opposite the present entrance to Clare. All that now survives is the lower part of the Gate, which is incorporated in the Old University Library. The court itself was begun in 1441 and demolished in 1836, but its appearance in the early nineteenth century is shown in Ackermann's aquatint.

Henry VI had intended a great court south of the chapel, and everybody for 275 years kept meaning to carry out the founder's intention. It nearly happened in 1602, when Ralph Symons, who built the famous second court of St. John's, was instructed to prepare designs ; but nothing came of it. It nearly happened again in 1636 and 1685, and very nearly indeed in 1713. In that year Wren, aged 80, was consulted, and he recommended his former assistant, Nicholas Hawksmoor. Hawksmoor produced two models, of which the second is quite admirable in the Roman manner, austere and simple, if heavy. This project too was dropped. But the building-fund opened in 1713 continued to increase, greatly helped by contributions from Sir Robert Walpole, an even more eminent Kingsman than his son Horace, and at last in 1723 the college took its courage in one hand (but not, unfortunately, in both) and placed the work in the hands of James Gibbs, architect of St. Martin's-in-the-Fields, who was already working on the Senate House.

The Gibbs or Fellows' Building, which extends southwards from the west end of the chapel, is by reason of its site and its scale one of the outstanding classical buildings in Cambridge. As its towering neighbour, the chapel, embodies the late fifteenth-century mind with all its aspirations and enthusiasms, the Gibbs Building shows perfectly the Augustan mind: immaculately correct, austerely rational and sufficiently elegant for the demands of good-breeding. It is not a romantic *tour de force*, but it is exceedingly good architecture.

The intention had been that this building should be one wing of a court, the side nearest the street where the screen now is to correspond with the existing Gibbs, and the south side, where the hall now is, to have an important Corinthian portico. The building fund, however, would not run to this, so that for another hundred years the college consisted of the chapel, the Old Court to the north and Gibbs to the south, though in 1784 a design was prepared by Adam. Then, in 1823, the front court was completed by William Wilkins.[1] As Mr Christopher Hussey has pointed out, Wilkins was soon after faced again with the problem of fitting himself into a scene dominated by Gibbs, when he built the National Gallery in proximity to St. Martin's Church.

[1] This is discussed in Chapter XI, where it is more appropriate.

DESCRIPTION

King's is a fortunate college, architecturally the most important in Cambridge or Oxford, set off by its two enormous lawns and the pleasant meadow of Scholar's Piece across the river, and with the faultless Clare for neighbour. King's from the Backs is one of the most celebrated views in the country, and perhaps nowhere in England can such a good architecture lesson be obtained as by contemplating from one spot the Renaissance Clare, the late-Gothic chapel, the Augustan Gibbs and the romantic Neo-Gothic Wilkins range. But that takes us too far away from the fifteenth century, and we must return to it at once.

To the south of King's and immediately adjacent on the river-front lies Queens', as near to it in date as it is topographically, and as different in character as it is in scale. The college is an odd mixture of the characteristic Cambridge collegiate style and the late mediæval manor-house. There is none of the great spaciousness of King's nor the formal beauty of Clare ; its appeal lies in the variety of its buildings within a small compass, in the contrast between red brick and black-and-white and in the various qualities that form the " Picturesque." The site is narrow and long, being bounded on the east, or entrance, side by Queens' Lane, which is the remains of Milne Street, on the south by Silver Street, leading to one of the two main traffic bridges over the river, and on the west by the river itself. The river-front of Queens' plays a most conspicuous part in the composite make-up of the Backs, which begin here, as they end at St. John's, with buildings rising straight out of the water. The effect is very Bruges.

When Queens' was founded in 1448 Andrew Doket became its President and held the office for forty years. The first court and Gate-house were completed by 1451 and are to-day exactly as they were then, except for the hideous belfry which disfigures the hall. The Gate is the earliest of that type in which Cambridge is so rich and was later followed by those of Jesus, Christ's, John's, and Trinity ; it retains its original solid wooden doors.

The second court is rather later and of various dates. The cloisters, which have an almost monastic effect, are, on the west side, of about 1460 and on the two lateral sides some thirty years later. The very celebrated black-and-white range on the north side is the President's Lodge and was built during the first half of the sixteenth century.

This is a jumble of varying units, unrelated to each other ; there are four different staircases, each of a different century, and none of the rooms is on the ground floor. It is exceedingly picturesque, though perhaps more suitable to a coaching-inn than to a college.

This range is the only timbered collegiate building to have survived, which is fortunate. Until 1911 the court side was covered with plaster of a pleasantly weathered texture, the removal of which, revealing the timber structure, did not meet with unanimous approval. The Long Gallery which was a regular feature of any big Elizabethan or Jacobean house is unusual in a college, though St. John's and Emmanuel each have one.

In the south-west corner, off the cloister court, is a small and rather depressing yard called Pump Court. The turret between this and the first court is traditionally where Erasmus kept during his embittered residence here. The severe classical block facing the river by the Silver Street bridge is by James Essex and, although in a rather unpleasing brick, introduces a very welcome and masculine note of architecture into the picturesque huddle of the rest.

The wooden bridge leading from the cloister court across the river to Queens' Grove is a very celebrated feature. It is, in fact, a copy of the original, which was accounted a great marvel of applied mathematics and soon got attributed to Sir Isaac Newton. As Newton died in 1727 and the bridge was originally constructed in 1749, this authorship seems unlikely. There is a distinct and pleasing flavour of chinoiserie about this engaging object.

To the north of the first court is Walnut Tree Court, leading to the remarkably good chapel built by Bodley in 1890 and the Friar's and Doket Buildings of 1886 and 1912. Connecting the chapel with the first court is a range built in 1617 which originally had the usual Jacobean gables, dormers, and steep-pitched roof; after a fire in 1778 the upper portion of this range was rebuilt and gothicised with battlements and hood-moulds.

On the opposite side of Queens' Lane to Queens' main front, and rather nearer to King's, is St. Catharine's (vulgarly, Cat's). Although this aspect is the back of the college, it will be more convenient to go in this way and walk through. In date it is very near to Queens', being in fact only six years younger, but it retains so little, if anything, of its original fabric that it is in effect a seventeenth-century building. For 220 years it remained small and poor, cramped in between Queens' Lane and the back of the inn called then The Black Bull, which was the ancestor of the Bull Hotel. In 1626 the property on which stood the Bull was bequeathed to St. Catharine's by an unpatriotic Caiusman, and the considerable increase of income enabled the college to rebuild. It will be more appropriate to discuss this in a later chapter.[1]

Now we must take a long walk, along King's Parade and past

[1] See Chapter X.

Great St. Mary's Church into Trinity Street. The University Church, after King's Chapel, is the best piece of late mediæval church architecture in Cambridge and a really excellent late Perpendicular work whose nave stands comparison with such famous East Anglian specimens as Lavenham and Saffron Walden. The chancel retains some survivals from the fourteenth century, but otherwise the church was almost wholly rebuilt between 1478 and 1519, though the top of the tower was not finished till late Elizabethan times and was finally embellished under James I. Above its stately arcades the nave retains its fine early Tudor timber roofs whose completion was helped by Henry VII.

We go on through Whewell's Court opposite the main buildings of Trinity, across Sidney Street and down Jesus Lane to Jesus, which we at last come to on the left. The approach to Jesus is along a depressing flagged path between high walls, which is known as " the Chimney." These walls conceal the Master's and Fellows' Gardens.

When Jesus was founded in 1496 it was near Cambridge, not in it. In fact, its remote and peaceful position caused James I to say that his ideal would be to pray at King's, dine at Trinity, and study and sleep at Jesus.

John Alcock, the Founder, was Bishop of Ely and, like Bishops Fisher and Fox, a prominent man of affairs. He set energetically to work on adapting, where possible, the buildings of the ancient nunnery of St Radegund and, where this was not possible, by building anew. First of all he increased the accommodation available in the main court by pulling down part of the nave of the conventual church, and by converting the main fabric of this nave into chambers. The refectory became, naturally, the hall, and this is unusual among Cambridge halls in being upstairs. Structurally it is very much as Alcock left it after his alterations, except for the wainscotting and the extremely elegant panelling, of 1703, behind the high table. On no account to be overlooked is a charming little Perpendicular oriel, almost like an eighteenth-century Gothic gazebo, which enabled the Master to spy on the behaviour of the undergraduates in hall.

In the cloister under the hall, just by the buttery, and on the East side of the cloister, are evident traces of the original nunnery ; the latter portion, somewhat battered, but highly cherished and recently repainted so as to show it more clearly, comprises the Early English entrance arches of the chapter-house.

The chapel is unusual, among Cambridge college chapels, in being cruciform. It is at once an important mediaeval building and an important item in the work of Pugin. It consists of the choir, crossing, tower, transepts, and a part of the nave of the convent church.

The north transept is of the twelfth century, and with its round-headed arches is exceedingly grand and impressive. The choir is of the early thirteenth century and its roof is by Pugin who restored it to its original. The four great tower arches are impressively simple and have a fine arcade above them.

The lancet windows have very interesting glass designed by Pugin, and the windows above the stalls were designed by Burne-Jones, though they were made by William Morris' company as late as 1914. The same company, in 1873–7, made the windows in the ante-chapel which were designed by Madox Brown and Burne-Jones. They have a great reputation, and the two on the north side at any rate deserve it. The very decorative adornment of the ceiling is also by William Morris. Taken all in all, this great building is of high importance both architecturally and for its decoration.

Apart from the chapel and cloister court, the most notable feature of Jesus is the main gate-tower, built by Alcock and rather an advance on the gate of Queens', fifty years earlier. Its proportions were completely spoilt, unfortunately, in 1718 when an extra storey was added to the two flanking ranges ; this makes it look more squat than it really is. The outer face of the tower has some exquisite detail and carving, not so rich as that at St. John's or Christ's, but very graceful. The side of the court opposite the gate-house is a Stuart imitation of early Tudor and was built in 1638 ; the back of this range has an unusual arrangement of chimney-stacks, which occur at regular intervals, with deep triangular projection, and form a most successful variation on the flat surface.

One of the surprising features of Jesus is quite a good building by Waterhouse ; that is to say, it is quite good by comparison with his work at Caius and Pembroke.

The spaciousness of the grounds is another surprise, giving it the same park-like appearance that Downing has. It opens on to the " serious " part of the river by the boat-houses belonging to the University and various college rowing-clubs.

The founding of Jesus closes the fifteenth century. The sixteenth opens with the founding and building of Christ's. To visit Christ's from Jesus entails walking back along Jesus Lane, turning to the left along Sidney Street, and continuing straight on to the junction of Petty Cury and St. Andrew's Street. Christ's occupies the corner site on the left. This also, in 1505, when the college was founded, was on the outskirts of the town.

As Jesus grew out of the nunnery of St. Radegund, and as Trinity grew out of Michaelhouse and King's Hall, so Christ's grew out of the small collegiate foundation of Godshouse, which originated on its present site in 1446. Sixty years later John Fisher drew the attention of his patroness, Lady Margaret Beaufort, to the already rather decrepit little Godshouse, with the result that Lady Margaret refounded and endowed it as Christ's. It was not, however, a suppression, but a merging, and the old was carried over into the new. The last Proctor of Godshouse, John Syclyng, became the first Master of Christ's, and the existing buildings were not all destroyed, but wherever possible adapted. There is some degree of antiquarian uncertainty as to which parts of the fabric to-day are original Godshouse and which were actually erected by Lady Margaret.

The chapel may perhaps incorporate some fragments of Godshouse, and certainly has some glass from its windows, but in the main it was built entirely anew, in early sixteenth-century Perpendicular, and was finished by the end of 1511. The brass eagle lectern, of about 1490, is a Godshouse survival. More notable are the excellent panelling and organ-case of 1702, and the fine monument of 1684 by Joseph Catterns to the joint memory of Sir John Finch and Sir Thomas Baines, who lived in David-and-Jonathan friendship from their undergraduate days in 1645 till the death of Baines in 1681 ; Finch died just over a year later.

The entrance to Christ's, at a rather confusing junction of streets, is through the great gate-tower. This, though not its flanking turrets, is the gate of Godshouse. The turrets were added later, and so was the magnificent display of stone heraldry on the street-front, with its Tudor crowned roses, Beaufort portcullises, Beaufort " Yales " or antelopes, and Lady Margaret's marguerites, which is clearly both a derivative from and a great elaboration of the decoration on the Gate of Jesus, and from which in turn derives the even more elaborate heraldry on the Gate of St. John's.

The rebuilding and adapting of the first court was completed by 1510. Apart from having been refaced and refenestrated in the eighteenth century, the court remains essentially the same in its arrangement. While the earlier Queens' and the later St. John's are both red brick, Christ's is a reversion to the local clunch stone of Corpus and Peterhouse. The hall was reconstructed by the younger Gilbert Scott in 1876, and the roof removed, reconstructed, and replaced.

Between the chapel and the hall lies the Master's Lodge, which is widely regarded as being the college's chief glory. The first floor was reserved for the use of Lady Margaret herself on her frequent visits to Cambridge and for Fisher in her absence. The Master had to put up with the ground-floor rooms. One of the most interesting objects is Lady Margaret's Oratory, on the first floor, which contains

51 Queen's : the President's Lodge from the Garden

52　Christ's : the Fellows' Building

53   St. John's :   the Combination Room

54   Magdalene : the Pepysian Library

a window looking directly into the chapel. This is unique in Cambridge and, as Sir Arthur Shipley said, recalls the window giving on to the chapel at the Escorial.

Sir Arthur Shipley, Master of Christ's, devoted himself between 1911 and 1920 to an extensive scheme for the strengthening and reconstruction of the Lodge, most of which he paid for out of his own pocket. In the course of these operations all manner of antiquarian oddments came to light, including fragments of what is probably the earliest English wallpaper, datable to 1509, and four mummified Old English black rats, who had died in a most scholarly nest consisting of fragments of a Caxton, a Wynkyn de Worde primer, four leaves of an otherwise unknown edition of Horace, some bits of fourteenth-century manuscripts and four playing-cards of about 1510, one for each rat. The Lodge also contains the famous bust of Milton by Pierce, which apart from the *ad vivum* engraving by Faithorne, is the only authentic portrait in his maturity. In the garden, which is particularly beautiful even for Cambridge, stands the so-called Milton's Mulberry-Tree ; Shipley has shown that it is likely to have been planted in 1608, the year of Milton's birth, but whether the " Lady of Christ's " was ever permitted to sit about under a tree in the Master's garden is quite another matter.

The real architectural glory of Christ's is the Fellows' Building, which is reached through the hall passage leading out of the first court. It was built between 1640 and 1642, and has a close affinity with the river-front of Clare by Robert Grumbold ; the evidence suggests that the Christ's building is by his slightly earlier kinsman Thomas Grumbold, who built Clare bridge. Evelyn called this building " a noble erection of very exact architecture " and meant exactly what he was saying. Even without its beautiful garden setting this would rank as one of the first-rate things in Cambridge.

Christ's and St. John's are far from being adjacent to one another, but in the dates and circumstances of their founding they are so closely allied that the visit to the latter must follow immediately that to the former. Leaving Christ's by the main gate and turning to the right, we must walk the length of Sidney Street, past Sidney Sussex, to St. John's Street, turning at a right-angle to the left opposite the Round Church. St. John's, unmistakable from its enormous Scott-Gothic chapel, is the first of that great series of neighbours which ends with the Fitzwilliam Museum, by way of Trinity, Great St. Mary's, King's, Corpus, St. Catharine's, the Pitt Press, Pembroke and Peterhouse, making the street even more remarkable than Oxford's High.

St. John's, or John's, as it is called, is above all things fortunate in its planning : three large courts and two noble gates on one axis-line, all in red brick (except for the chapel and the south side of the first court) ; and across the river the abrupt and happy contrast of the new buildings. Lady Margaret had been able personally to oversee most of the works at Christ's before her death in 1509, but St. John's is the work of Fisher, as her executor, and the first court was built under his direct supervision between 1510 and 1516. Until about 1775 this court was entirely uniform, but then the south side was refaced with ashlar and assumed its present appearance. Homogeneity was finally, destroyed in 1863 when the original chapel, the first part of the college to be built and partly that of the old Hospital, was pulled down and the present monstrous church was erected. It had in fact been decided to build a new chapel as far back as 1687, when Robert Grumbold had produced a model, but unfortunately the scheme was shelved for 175 years. There is no knowing what Grumbold's design was like, but if it were as good as his work elsewhere it must join Essex's projected court at Corpus as one of the most regretted architectural " ifs " of Cambridge. As it is, Scott's " Early Decorated " structure is good of its kind, but it is quite the wrong kind ; admirable as a large parish church, it is not only hopelessly out-of-place at St. John's but quite unsuited for a college chapel anywhere. It is one of the most unpopular buildings in Cambridge, nearly as much so as Waterhouse's block at Caius.

The gate-tower is even more magnificent than that of Christ's, with heraldic carving even more elaborate. The dignity of this noble gate makes the new chapel look uncommonly foolish and inappropriate. The hall has a remarkable and much-admired linenfold screen, and the passage between hall and buttery still has its elaborate contemporary ceiling and a doorway which repeats the heraldic carving of the gate.

This screens passage leads into the second court, which was built by Ralph Symons chiefly at the expense of Mary Cavendish, Countess of Shrewsbury, between 1598 and 1602, ninety years after the first, and which doubled the size of the college. It is really the result of rivalry with its great and growing neighbour, Trinity. In the contract it was laid down that this new court should be as nearly as possible " answerable to the owlde buildinge " with the result that it is really late-Elizabethan imitating early-Tudor. It is extremely successful as an example of regular and perfect uniformity, and, placed symmetrically on the axial line of the college, it is a beautiful bit of planning, as Ruskin pointed out. By contrast the third court, though still on the main axis, is a picturesque muddle. The Combination Room, on the first floor of the second court, is far the most important Elizabethan interior in Cambridge, and at night, with the enchantment of candle-light and silver-plate, can look extremely romantic.

A gate-tower, more humbly repeating the first, leads into the third court which was built at two different periods and, except for being of red brick, makes no attempt to harmonise with the two existing courts. First of all, the north range was built by 1624, to house the library, at the expense of the princely Archbishop and Lord-Keeper Williams. Then the south and west ranges were added between 1670 and 1674. They are not only distinct from the other two sides, but quite distinct from each other. The river aspect of this court is pure Picturesque in the eighteenth-century meaning of that word; disordered, asymetrical and romantic, with a muddle of gables and projections and recessions, in a mixture of Gothic and Renaissance. It is odd that this picturesque disorder should be thirty years later than the first Court of Clare and the Fellows' Building of Christ's; evidently St. John's had never heard of Inigo Jones. The puzzling initials I.L.C.S. on one of the gables are those of Lord-Keeper Williams, at that time Bishop of Lincoln : *Johannes Lincolniensis Custos Sigilli.*

The college had, however, heard of Wren, to whom the very beautiful Old Bridge is often attributed. There is some reason for this, as it has been shown that Wren was consulted and that he sent drawings, and there is a considerable correspondence in which Wren proposed to straighten-out the river where it bends sharply near Trinity Library ; not surprisingly, this scheme was found to be a little too expensive. In fact, the so-called " Wren's Bridge " was built by Robert Grumbold, helped by a Wren design ; that is to say, a design prepared in Wren's office. Begun in 1696, it and the noble gate-piers which lead on to it were finished by 1712. In addition to their own beauty, they serve to stabilise and pull together the confusion of the third court.

The building of the bridge finished off the college in a complete and regular plan, covering the whole area between St. John's Street and the river. And so it remained till 1830, when the new bridge and the new buildings across the river were built. These new buildings, however, are so completely distinct from the rest of the college and are in themselves so important that it is more appropriate to discuss them later on.[1]

[1] See Chapter XI.

IX   Reformation Cambridge

CHRIST'S AND ST. JOHN'S, THOUGH BOTH WERE BUILDING AT the beginning of Henry VIII's reign, are legacies of Lady Margaret and owe nothing either directly or indirectly to her grandson.   Apart from these two, the sixteenth century saw the founding of four colleges: Magdalene, Trinity, Emmanuel and Sidney Sussex, and the refounding of Caius.

These five are widely separated from each other, Magdalene and Emmanuel being about as far from each other as any two colleges in Cambridge, except perhaps Peterhouse and Jesus.   So on leaving John's it is best to go first to Magdalene, which one does by walking back towards the Round Church, turning left along Bridge Street and crossing the river by the Great Bridge.   The main part of Magdalene is then on the right with its modern buildings across the street on the left.

Magdalene, as we have seen, is now in its third form of existence.   Originally a hostel founded by the Fenland Abbeys of Ely, Crowland, Ramsey, and Walden, it grew during the fifteenth century into Buckingham College, but was still monastic; that is to say, it remained an offshoot of Crowland Abbey and when that abbey was dissolved under Henry VIII Buckingham College was also dissolved.   The property, together with that of Walden, was bestowed on a deserving and submissive Lord Chancellor, Thomas Lord Audley, and in 1542 was refounded by him as Magdalene.

As the college now stands the side of the first court nearest to the street is a survival of the original hostel, five staircases and their entrance-doors dating from between 1425 and 1450, though they have been much refaced and are largely hidden by an excessive growth of vegetation.   The chapel represents the next phase, the Buckingham College period, having been built by the second Duke of Buckingham about 1480.   It was, however, completely altered in the mid-eighteenth century into an elegant Italianate affair with a flat roof, and it was made Gothic again in the last century.   The third Duke of Buckingham is said to have erected the hall about

55 Trinity : the Library from the Backs

56   Trinity : the Interior of the Library

1519, but it is now to all appearances a Queen Anne interior; in place of the original high open roof there is a flat ceiling, and there is a very unusual and elaborate gallery at the buttery end, which rather resembles a stage-setting in some small and intimate theatre. Both the hall and the combination-room have admirable panelling, the latter being later and dating from 1757. The panelling in the guest-room is Jacobean, but was installed there in 1916, having been bought from the old post office in Magdalene Street opposite the front gate.

Magdalene has long had a reputation for good food and for doing itself well, so that the traditional translation of the motto over the hall entrance " Garde ta Foye " as " Mind your Liver " has a practical if not a philological justification.

The farther, or hall, range of the first court is pierced by the screens passage which leads through to the library court. This pleasant, though slightly amateurish and asymmetrical, library was begun about probably 1670, though not completed till some thirty years later. It is not of special architectural importance, but it houses Samuel Pepys' library, which came to the college from Pepys' nephew in 1724, the date rather misleadingly inscribed on the front of this seventeenth-century building. The books stand in the same order in the same presses of 1666 as when they were in Pepys' house in London, and the presses themselves are very fine indeed. Pepys took a great and justifiable pride in them, as indeed he did in the collection itself which includes a respectable number of important items, both printed and MS., and of course the cypher manuscript of the famous Diary. Magdalene is one of the smallest colleges, although it has so often attracted numbers of smart and fashionable young men.

Trinity, in its present form founded four years later in 1546, is by a very long way the biggest of all the colleges and is officially the most important—that is to say, the Assize Judge is lodged in it when on circuit; Royalty goes up to it as an undergraduate; and its Master-ship is the position of highest eminence in either University. Its buildings and courts cover an immense area, but unfortunately its architectural distinction is not high, with one exception : Nevile's Court is admirable and the Library, which closes its west end, is one of Wren's most distinguished early designs.

Walking back from Magdalene, past St. John's again, the Great Gate of Trinity, perpetually hedged in term-time by a tangle of male and female bicycles, stands back from Trinity Street on the right, adorned half-way up by a dissipated-looking effigy of Henry VIII. This gate differs from St. John's, Christ's, and the others by having two portals on the cat-and-kitten principle, one small and one large. Beyond this gate stretches the immense expanse of the Great Court. On the right, or north side, is the chapel and beyond it on the same side as the hall, the Master's Lodge. On the far side opposite to the main gate, the west side, is the hall and on the left, or south, side is Queen's Gate, leading through to Bishop's Hostel, Garret Hostel Lane, and Trinity Hall. The screens passage by the hall leads through to Nevile's Court, the Library and the river, and on the left of Nevile's Court is New Court.

Henry VIII is regarded as Trinity's founder, as indeed he was. He brought his great new college into being by the suppression of Michaelhouse and King's Hall as separate and independent foundations and their amalgamation, with St. Gregory's and Physick Hostels, into one college. Several of the existing buildings were taken over and that pretty well determined the new lay-out.

The Great Gate, without the tower and turrets, was begun in 1519 as the gate of King's Hall; it was completed in 1525. This gate became the main entrance to the new college and was taken as the north-east corner of the new Great Court. But a more important part of King's Hall is King Edward's Gate, now on the north side of the Great Court just west of the chapel. Built about 1426–30, it has quite a different character to the later and heavier Great Gate. It originally stood well to the south of its present site, out towards what is now the middle of the court, and was shifted in 1600. Till then—that is to say, until the end of the sixteenth century—the court was only about half its present size. There are other fragments of King's Hall in the small and very pretty garden-court to the north-west of the chapel, behind King Edward's Gate, which is generally locked as it is the Fellows' bowling green.

In 1593 Thomas Nevile became master and took seriously in hand the matter of building. He was determined to make Trinity the biggest and most important college in the place, and was in the end able to best his neighbour, the Master of St. John's, who had exactly the same ambition for his own college. Nevile built the great hall and kitchen, pushed back King Edward's Gate, built the Queen's Gate on the south side, completed the court on its present scale, built the famous fountain in the middle and extended the college westwards by laying out Nevile's Court. His architect was Ralph Symons, whom we have already encountered at St. John's and King's.

The Great Court is, of course, the best-known court in the whole of Cambridge, principally because it is the biggest. It is widely admired, but its admirers are chiefly those who appear to confuse extent with excellence, like Nevile himself. It has little character, beyond what is given it by its size, and if it were not for the Fountain it would have even less. This celebrated object was built in 1602, and by its very skilful placing and rightness of scale serves quite admirably as the one co-ordinating factor in the whole lay-out. It is essential that the Fountain be regarded in this light as well as in the light of its intrinsic merit as a late-Elizabethan conceit; from every angle it takes the eye, and almost prevents one noticing how small and unimpressive are the surrounding buildings when compared with the vast area they enclose. But in the south-west corner, that farthest from the main gate, is the one piece of serious architecture in the court, a block classically refronted by Essex in 1774. Like his block on the river-front at Queens', it gives a note of distinction and authority to an undistinguished conglomeration, but for that very reason may perhaps appear more important than it actually is.

The chapel was already built before Nevile's time. It is a dull building, with the rarity value of being one of the very few ecclesiastical buildings of the reign of Mary I. The great *baldachino* at the east end and the panelling are early Georgian, and manage to redeem the chapel from complete lifelessness. The ante-chapel is much more interesting than the chapel by reason of the famous Newton statue of 1755 by Roubiliac.

With the hall and the gargantuan kitchen we return to Nevile. He built these in 1604–5 and thereby completed his Great Court. The old hall of Michaelhouse had stood to the south of the present hall; part of its site became the kitchen and part of it became the Combination Room in the block refaced by Essex. The roof of Nevile's hall is a curious Jacobean version of the traditional hammer-beam construction, and does not stand a very close inspection. It is too thin and flimsy for its scale and, being full of a deal of pointless Jacobean ornamentation, it quite misses the structural emphasis of the real thing. The woodwork of the screens and gallery is wildly elaborate, in the Jacobean manner, and the lovers of the intricate find it as fascinating as the screen in King's chapel.

The insatiable Nevile next set out to build the entirely new court that bears his name between the hall and the river. Access to this is by the usual screens passage between hall and buttery.

The original design of Nevile's Court may have been Symons's, but as he died in 1605 he cannot have supervised the building, which was finished in 1615. The essential feature of the court is the ranges of chambers carried above open loggias by arcading. As Nevile left it, the court was gabled and had sloping roofs with dormer-windows, probably very like Symons's second court at St. John's. The west end, towards the river, was closed merely by a wall with a gate in it, and the whole area was about half that of the present court.

It remained like this till the Mastership of Isaac Barrow, who in 1675 decided to build a Library to close the court. Barrow was an old friend of Christopher Wren, so naturally and very fortunately Wren became architect of the new Library which was begun in the following year. He gave his services free.

It must be remembered that at that time the Backs, as we know them in their present beauty, did not exist. The river was simply a highway for barges to and from Lynn; therefore the river-front of the Library was not regarded by Wren as the most important aspect; the court, or east, front was for him the most important. He set his building back near the river, the sides of the court being lengthened, and repeated the colonnade. As this long façade has no central feature, he set four statues on the centre of the roof-line to give the necessary emphasis; they are by Caius Gabriel Cibber, and are most excellently placed. The river, or west, aspect which was not meant to be scrutinised so carefully is in fact the one that is most widely familiar. In its simplicity and precision it is perfect architecture, by a man who always knew exactly what he wanted to do and, in this case at any rate, when to stop. He has stressed the length and horizontality of his front, but the three admirable portals counteract any tendency towards over-stressing of this.

The interior of the Library is magnificent. It is very long, but never tedious, and the four corner alcoves are particularly happy. The heraldic wood-carvings on the ends of the book-presses are all but one by Grinling Gibbons himself, who carved them between 1691 and 1693. A double line of busts, several of them by Roubiliac, leads up to the famous statue of Byron by Thorwaldsen at the end. This was executed in 1829, sent to England in 1834 to be placed in Westminster Abbey, refused admittance by the Dean, and buried in the cellars of the Customs House for nine years till it was rescued by the original subscribers and presented to Trinity. The great south window behind it is a very interesting piece of eighteenth-century stained glass, good examples of which are not too plentiful in England. It was made by William Peckitt of York in 1775 from designs by Cipriani, and compares very well with the windows on the north side of New College Chapel, Oxford, also made by Peckitt.[1] The Trinity window represents the noble and appropriate subject

[1] See Walpole Society, Vol. XVII, 1928–29.

of Sir Isaac Newton being presented to George III by Cantabrigia, with Fame, Britannia, and Sir Francis Bacon in attendance.

Returning down into Nevile's Court one is faced at the opposite, or east, end of the court by another piece of Wren's work, in the form of a balustraded terrace or " tribune " with two flights of steps leading into the court from the screens passage. It is a pretty object and serves to ease the abrupt transition from the Gothic hall to the Renaissance court.

The court took on its present appearance in 1755, when it became necessary to reconstruct it. The work was done by James Essex, and the changes were drastic ; they were also improvements. The ranges on both sides, which at different times had been brought nearly to the Library, were increased in height, the sloping roofs, gables and dormers were abolished, a balustrade was added to the top all round, and the court was finally extended westwards so as to meet the library. Each side is separately very satisfactory, but the most frequent criticism is that the junction of each side with the library is awkward, which is certainly true.

Returning through into the Great Court we have the Queen's Gate on the right. Beyond this, that is to say behind the south-west corner of Great Court on the old site of Garret Hostel, is a charming red-brick building of 1670, known as Bishop's Hostel after Bishop Hackett of Lichfield, in the design of which it is thought that Wren may have had a hand. This house is always rather a surprise, since its character is so much more domestic than collegiate.

We will leave Trinity's nineteenth-century additions till later, and move along to its neighbour, Caius, which lies to the south, on the right of Trinity Street going towards King's. By its original foundation in 1348 as Gonville Hall it is the third surviving college in the University, but its present scale and importance and, indeed, its whole character date from its refounding as Gonville and Caius in 1557. During its earliest years, Gonville Hall was a miserable little institution behind St. Botolph's Church. It was removed to its present site in 1351, but continued to be small and miserable, even more so after Physick Hostel was snatched from it by Henry VIII and incorporated in Trinity. This deplorable state was completely remedied when Dr. Caius set about it. First of all, he planned Caius Court with its entrance on the lane running down past the Old Schools to Clare ; it was, as it still is, an open, three-sided court, so designed by Caius for the sake of fresh air, and was then an innovation which at later periods was repeated at Emmanuel, Sidney Sussex, King's, and St. Catharine's, though the reasons were different.

Leading into Caius Court from the lane is the Gate of Honour, and leading out of it on the east side into the first court is the Gate of Virtue. The former dates from 1573, the latter from 1567, and a third, the Gate of Humility, now stands in the Master's Garden much altered. These gates are great architectural curiosities and are such very early English Renaissance that there are still traces of Tudor Gothic here and there about them. To us they are architectural toys, but Dr. Caius certainly built them in no spirit of whimsy. They are, in fact, excellent specimens of symbolism, the Elizabethan's favourite pursuit, and they symbolise the successive stages along the academic path. The Gate of Honour, particularly, is built in the then latest mode of sophistication, making great play with the Orders in the fashionable-scholarly manner. The Georgian of, say, 1760 when building a similar series of toys would not, like Caius, have used the most modern idiom but would have fashionably imitated the past, and gone Gothick.

North of Caius Court, beyond the chapel, is Gonville Court. The college had increased in numbers since the days of Caius, but very little additional building had been done till Sir James Burrough, the Master, took it in hand in 1751. Burrough, as we have seen, was an amateur architect of high distinction, and has left his mark very noticeably on Cambridge: as noticeably as Symonds and the Grumbolds before him and Essex and Wilkins later. His genuinely improving hand is seen in the courts of Trinity Hall and Peterhouse as well as in his own college, and at Queens' and Clare, the Senate House, and Great St. Mary's. Between 1751 and 1753 he refaced the classical sides of Gonville Court in his usual sound and excellent taste, with an uncommonly pretty lantern over the west range.

Caius in the nineteenth century was again much enlarged. The hall was built by Anthony Salvin in 1853, and can offend nobody. But in 1868 Waterhouse built the gigantic and hopelessly overpowering block at the junction of Trinity Street and King's Parade. So much has been written about this, sometimes in anger, sometimes in derision, but never in praise, that there is nothing left to say. Caius men have as much reason for reviling the name of Waterhouse as have Pembroke men. The horror of this first court inside is considerably mitigated by the little avenue of limes across it. This is a very unusual feature, but Loggan's engravings show that many colleges had such avenues or rows across a court.

Caius has recently extended to the other side of Trinity Street, but these buildings are better discussed later on. We must return to the sixteenth century and to Emmanuel, which entails a longish walk either along King's Parade to Pembroke and up the whole length of Downing Street, which is heavy with scientific research, or else across the Market Hill and along Petty Cury and St. Andrew's Street, which has a much more town than gown atmosphere.

Emmanuel, however, is really best seen when being approached from the station. Most taxi-drivers take the St. Andrew's Street route into the town, and Emmanuel is the first college one sees after the dreary station purlieus. It welcomes one charmingly with a most agreeable grass and flower border along its street-front, which is always full of colour.

The college stands on the site of a Dominican Friary, which was of course dissolved by Henry VIII and of which very little now remains. The property after passing through various hands was bought by Sir Walter Mildmay with the express purpose of founding on it a college which should be a nursery for Puritan clergy. Mildmay was a big business man, at that time in his early sixties and immensely rich. He was of strongly Puritan opinions, but was careful not to be too extreme in their expression. Even so, Elizabeth I had her doubts about the new foundation, as we have already seen.

The buildings were begun in 1584 with Ralph Symons as architect. This is his first appearance in Cambridge architecture and led to his extensive employment at Sidney Sussex, Trinity, St. John's and, abortively, King's. The whole of Mildmay's original plan was completed before his death in 1589, but it was vastly different from the college's present form. The main entrance was then to the north, in Emmanuel Lane, and the main court was to the north, or left, of the present court; it was three-sided and open like that at Caius. Two passages led southwards past the Master's Lodge and the hall into what was then the inner and is now the main court, and the east side of this, where now stand the chapel and cloister, was open, making this court also three-sided.

It can be claimed that Mildmay's original hall remains, but it has been altered to an extent that practically amounts to a new hall, which we will look at later. The old chapel also more or less remains, though it is now a lecture-room. Mildmay's Puritanism ignored any pedantic correctness in the orientation of the chapel, which lay defiantly north and south; his Puritanism also disinclined him to use the perfectly sound Friary Church for his chapel and caused him to convert it into the hall.

The south, or right-hand, side of the present main court is called the Founder's Range, and was built in its original form by Symons, completing the college as Mildmay planned it. The college possesses a portrait of its founder, of course, but it also possesses one of Symons which has been claimed to be the earliest English portrait of an architect.

The first extension of Emmanuel came in 1633, with the range which lies southward from the far end of the Founder's Range. Apart from dormer-windows, which have disappeared, the building retains its original form, which is agreeable enough and looks well in its garden surroundings. The Harvard Room is in this range.

Emmanuel, naturally enough, enjoyed the period of the Common-wealth very much indeed. With the Restoration its hopes were rather dashed and it had to resign itself to becoming just one of the smaller colleges. Nevertheless, between 1667 and 1677 it suddenly occupied an important place in architectural history, through the happy association of two great men : William Sancroft and Chris-topher Wren. Sancroft had been Master till 1665 and then became Dean of St. Paul's. During the tremendous business of rebuilding the cathedral after the Fire, Sancroft found time to turn his attention to the improvement of his college, and, since Wren was at hand, Wren was to be employed. It has been suggested also that Sancroft had his eye on Wren already a few years earlier, during his actual mastership, when Wren was building Pembroke Chapel for his uncle, the Bishop of Ely.

Sancroft caused Wren to abandon Mildmay's chapel and build a new one, correctly orientated, across the open end of the then inner court. The result is an extremely elegant little chapel, with a good plaster ceiling by John Grove, who also modelled the one at Pem-broke, and a fine, swagger, sophisticated altar-painting by G. Amigoni. The outside view of the chapel is odd, because right across its west end and indeed right across the court runs the Long Gallery, which Wren built on an arcade. The effect is exceedingly pretty, though a trifle like an enlarged toy, and it would really be much better without the overpowering lantern, which is almost big enough to be a cupola. The Long Gallery is the last of its kind in Cambridge, and contains some good portraits, including a couple of Gainsborough bishops.

But the most distinguished part of Emmanuel is what was originally the Founder's Range and is now the Westmoreland Building, the right, or south, side of the main court. This range was entirely rebuilt in 1719–22 and given its present form. The architect's name is not certainly known, but it is thought that he, or rather they, may have been amateurs, two Fellows called Whitaker and Whitehead ; whoever was responsible, he or they have produced one of the most distinguished Georgian façades in Cambridge, a perfectly propor-tioned and perfectly fenestrated flat front whose central feature of two urn-topped pilasters is just sufficiently emphatic. This beauti-

57   Trinity : Nevile's Arcade ; alterations by Essex above

58   Trinity : a Grinling Gibbons Panel in the Library

60 Trinity: the Hall

59 Trinity: the Chapel

fully satisfying range is slightly marred by an awkward point of contact with the south end of the Long Gallery and cloister.

Then, of course, the rest of the court had to be dealt with, now that it had a Renaissance east side and a Georgian south one. So James Essex, rightly and properly, was called in. Cambridge was really very lucky in having, for a large part of the eighteenth century, two such sound and admirable architects to be made use of as Burrough and Essex. At Emmanuel Essex transformed the hall into its present form in 1760–4, with good, simple panelling and classical screens at either end. Just before this date Burrough had been approached in the matter of a design for the west, or St. Andrew's Street, front of the college, but nothing had come of it though Burrough had produced a scheme. Then in 1770 the work was put in Essex's hands, and the result was the main front as we see it now. It meant that the whole college was switched round from having its main entrance on to Emmanuel Lane to having it now in St. Andrew's Street, so that the former inner or second court became the main court. Essex's street-front is good, plain every-day Ionic, and has no fanciful tricks, partly because Essex did not approve of fanciful tricks and partly because he did not wish to distract attention from Wren's work across the court. It is not spectacular, but it is dignified and a great improvement on the makeshift Friary survival which had stood there till then.

The original entrance in Emmanuel Lane is now occupied by a range in 1825 Gothic, dull, plain stucco with good proportions, and across the lane is the new North Court, built in 1913.

Emmanuel's gardens, with the Paddock in addition, are really notable, and astonishingly spacious. In fact, Emmanuel really has all the qualities of architecture and gardening that one generally associates with one of the greater colleges. As it is, it rather tends to get overlooked, perhaps because it is such a long way from everywhere.

It is admittedly rather a long way from Sidney Sussex, which is the next college in date. One walks along St. Andrew's Street, past Christ's, and along Sidney Street, and on the right are the charming mock-Gothic buildings of the little college whose one great distinction is to have been the nursery of Oliver Cromwell.

Sidney, in its present shape, is so entirely 1820 that it must be considered in relation to the *faux-Gothique* parts of King's and St. John's. Its earlier history is quite briefly told. As we have already seen, it was founded in 1596 by Lady Frances Sidney, Countess of Sussex, on the site of the dissolved Grey Friars. The architect was, as usual at that time in Cambridge, Ralph Symons, and the buildings, including the chapel, were completed by 1600. It then consisted of the present north, or left-hand, court and was of dark-red brick, probably rather too high for the small space enclosed, and must have been distinctly inferior to St. John's. On the east side, farthest from the street, was and still is the hall, and the side nearest the street was open except for a brick wall and a tremendously elaborate gate which, according to Loggan's engraving, embodied nearly all the favourite Elizabethan conceits and fancies.

Then, about twenty-five years later, another little open, three-sided court was built to the south of the first, so that the college took the form which it still has, an E with its three arms abutting on the street, forming two adjacent open courts. The eighteenth century saw various alterations, mostly due to Symons' buildings being on the point of falling down, as at Trinity also. They were certainly ruinous by 1730, and the gate either fell down or was taken away in 1749. The classical gate which replaced it was in turn removed, and now forms the entrance to the Master's Garden round the corner in Jesus Lane.

Then the hall was agreeably Italianised and a flat ceiling placed beneath the open roof, and in 1776 the old chapel was pulled down and a new one subsequently erected—of course by Essex again. But the chapel interior as it now is dates from just before 1914. It is in the classic tradition, but is over-enriched for its size, and there really are too many carved wooden canopies about. The reticence of, for example, Clare Chapel is markedly absent.

Finally, in 1821, the college began to assume its present charming form, or rather the form which would be charming if one could see it through the creeper which envelopes it.

The founding of Sidney coincides with the end of the sixteenth century. No more colleges were built until Downing was started in 1807, but the seventeenth century saw a certain amount of rebuilding and remodelling.

61   Emmanuel : the Westmoreland Building

64   King's: the Gibbs Building and Chapel

65 Clare · the River Front

X   Seventeenth-Century and Georgian Cambridge

NTELLECTUALLY, THE SEVENTEENTH CENTURY IN CAMBRIDGE HAS two great moments, with the Cambridge Platonists in the 'sixties and Newton at the end ; but it lacks the sustained brilliance of the sixteenth century.   Architecturally it has also two great moments, with Clare and St. Catharine's, but it has not stamped so deep an impression on the place as have the eighteenth and early nineteenth centuries.   No colleges were founded, no great public buildings erected.   Most colleges have a piece of seventeenth-century— sometimes of the highest distinction, like Christ's Fellows' Building and the Wren work at Pembroke, Emmanuel, and Trinity ; some- times of a slightly less important degree, like Peterhouse Chapel, the so-called " Wren " bridge at St. John's, and the Carolean Range at Emmanuel ; sometimes merely picturesque affairs, like the Library at Magdalene (which only just fails to be better than that) or the third court at St. John's.   Wren and Grinling Gibbons added beauty to several of the colleges ; they are European figures and bestowed their gifts on Oxford equally.

Cambridge is a *locus classicus* for a select group of architects who, while they worked elsewhere also, are best seen there.   Ralph Symons at the end of the sixteenth, the Grumbold kinsmen in the seventeenth, James Essex and James Burrough in the eighteenth, and William Wilkins in the nineteenth century.   We have met all these in almost every college we have visited.   But we have not yet visited Clare.

Clare, like King's, is fortunate in its site.   It contributes to and is an integral part of one of the most memorable architectural experiences to be had in England ; a great part of its beauty derives from the immense, smooth expanse of the Lawn of King's, the appropriate and artificial foreground to a very sophisticated façade ;

another part of its beauty derives from the Backs ; but most of all its excellence is intrinsic.

Clare is nearly of the same early date as Corpus, so far as its founding is concerned. But no farther than that. Unlike Corpus or Peterhouse, it retains nothing of its original buildings. After successive fires the remains of the mediæval buildings were finally pulled down before the middle of the seventeenth century. While the old Corpus has an antiquarian interest and a degree of associational charm, the new Clare has a quite extraordinary architectural distinction. The usual thing is to compare it with a Renaissance palace, and it certainly has a palace air about it ; the side towards King's could well have been a residence of Charles I and is far more courtly than Whitehall (despite the Banqueting House) ever was. When one stands on King's bridge it is not difficult to imagine Clare and the Gibbs Building of King's freezing King's Chapel into the background, coming the aristocratic and the scholarly over the persistent romantic, as Horace Walpole and Evelyn might have come it over Charles Fox . . . if they could have sufficiently ignored chronology and if Charles Fox had tried to chdiscuss aritecture.

The building of Clare as we know it began shortly before 1640, and this phase, which ended with the outbreak of the Civil War, includes the south and east sides of the court and the famous bridge across the river ; that is, as one enters from Trinity Hall Lane in the corner by the west end of King's Chapel behind the Old Schools, the entrance and left-hand ranges. The inside of the north, or entrance, range is a little bit marred by the anachronism of the rather Germanic gateway, which harks back to early Renaissance and even with its fan-vaulted roof to late Perpendicular.[1] Although at this time the court had only two complete sides, the bridge was added. It is an uncommonly pretty object, marrying perfectly with the " Wren " bridge farther down at St. John's, and has the subtle and very effective trick of its balusters being set diagonally on their bases. It is by Thomas Grumbold.

The second phase of the building is post-restoration. The west side, opposite the gate, is by Thomas Grumbold's nephew Robert, begun in 1669 and finished by 1715. The river-front of this range is particularly distinguished and, since it is rather screened by trees, is best seen in winter. The north side of the court was begun later and finished earlier. Grumbold's Tower, on the north side of this north range, is a red-brick affair of considerable charm which verges

[1] One of the last examples of this taste, 1638, being a trifle later than the example at Christchurch, Oxford.

67 Clare : the Chapel

66 Clare : the Hall

68 The Senate House

69   The Senate House

70　The Old Schools: Library Front

on the quaint. In the library, which is of 1690, there is a rather unhappy marriage between the good proportions which that period would naturally produce and the Jacobean bookcases which have survived from an earlier building. But the chapel of the 1760's which is by Sir James Burrough and Essex, contains little except some nineteenth-century windows to mar its admirable simplicity and good taste ; Burrough may have been an amateur, but he shows in all his work that he had learnt the difficult art of saying as little as possible. He really is a man of most excellent and certain taste. One of the few occasions when he allows himself to be a little unusual and to play for effect is here, in the octagonal ante-chapel, and he has brought it off very well, though it is perhaps too lofty for its area.

The very fine wrought-iron gates and gateway on the Backs road, which date from 1714, lead across to the new building by Sir Giles Gilbert Scott, which are better discussed in relation with other modern buildings and not with the exquisite manners and well-bred dignity of the main court. So we will not go across but return through the court, up the passage by the Old Schools and Senate House into King's Parade, and along past King's to St. Catharine's.

St. Catharine's, as we have seen, is by foundation a daughter of King's, of the mid-fifteenth century. For 200 years the college was small, cramped and poor, but in 1674 a fortunate bequest enabled it to start rebuilding itself entirely. St. Catharine's has always been one of the obscurer colleges, but it is very good to look at, and a beautiful example of Restoration brick-building.

As at Clare, the rebuilding was complete, and it was even longer drawn-out. The central block, built by Robert Grumbold, was begun in 1674 and work went on till 1687 when the funds, always precarious, became exhausted. Then it began again in 1694 with the north or right-hand side, including the chapel, again by Grumbold ; and in 1704 it stopped again. In 1757 the south side was completed by Essex, who practically reproduced the design of the chapel.

This was a great and rather rare compliment on the part of Essex, who here showed the same deference to Grumbold as he did to Wren at Emmanuel. Grumbold is generally described as a provincial architect not much advanced beyond the mason—or builder—stage from which his uncle Thomas had just emerged ; but at Clare he showed himself very much an architect, and at St. Catharine's he did it again. The central feature of the centre block, for instance, is a stone-faced portal with an elliptical pediment, which not only possesses considerable dignity but also serves to set-off and emphasise the brick quality of the rest. Similarly, the entrance to the chapel

11*

is excellent architecture, obviously by a man who knew what he was about. The chapel itself is unusually lofty for its area, the rich little ante-chapel being much lower. This north side of the court displays the surprising feature of an oriel of 1868 and other windows with Victorian Perpendicular tracery.

These two colleges are the only two large-scale groups of seventeenth-century building in Cambridge and, numerically speaking, there is not really a great deal else when compared with the eighteenth and nineteenth centuries. Trinity's Wren Library is, with King's Chapel, one of the two focal points of the university : Christ's Fellows' Building is, after that and Clare, the best example of the century ; Pembroke and Emmanuel chapels have the great historic interest of being early Wren, though if they were not they might conceivably be less highly thought of. And, for the rest, there are the charming chapel at Peterhouse ; the 1633 range at Emmanuel ; the interesting 1638 range at Jesus ; the Magdalene Library of 1670 ; and the Third Court and " Wren " bridge at St. John's, which between them cover the years from the 1620's to the 1690's.

Georgian Cambridge, by contrast with Stuart Cambridge, made up in architectural activity whatever it may have lacked in intellectual liveliness ; though in that respect it was far from slothful while Bentley or Porson were about. We have already looked at most of the eighteenth-century buildings, and have almost everywhere encountered Messrs. Burrough and Essex. But there remain to be seen the University Old Library and the Senate House, and the belated Downing College.

The Old Library and the Senate House form that extremely elegant and Georgian group facing King's Parade between King's and Caius. The one nearest King's, facing towards the street, is the Old Library and that with its end to the street is the Senate House, where, amongst other ceremonies, degrees are conferred on undergraduates and honorary degrees on the eminent. The functions jointly performed by these two buildings have been performed on the same site since the early fifteenth century ; or, more accurately, on the site of the Old Library. Originally this was partly the Schools and partly the Regent House, seat of university government. Gradually a University library was accumulated, and was housed in the same building. From the time of Elizabeth I's Archbishop Parker onwards the growing library tended to swamp the other activities, until in 1719 it was decided to build a separate Senate House ; in 1754-8 a new façade, the present one, was clapped on to the library. After various extensions westwards, towards Clare, the entire library was moved in 1934 to the University New Library across the river, and the Old Library reverted to what was one of its original functions, housing the administrative offices which had been banished to the popular shopping-centre, St. Andrew's Street.

The Old Schools Quadrangle was probably finished by 1475, and the South Room on the first floor with its original wooden roof is of 1470. The North Room, until 1934 the Catalogue Room, is of the same date, but the plaster ceiling is Elizabethan of 1600. This was the Regent House until 1730. The main front of the library, late fifteenth century again, faced on to King's Parade (then called High Street) and is shown in an engraving by Loggan ; it remained more or less intact until 1754, when the present front was stuck on.

Expansion of the library was a constant problem. To the south lay King's Chapel, to the west King's Old Court, to the north Senate House Passage and Caius, and to the east the then High Street. The new Senate House relieved the congestion a little, and the purchase of the Old Court from King's for £12,000 in 1829 allowed considerable extension westwards. But at that moment a controversy broke out as to the use to which that site should be put. Some demanded that it should be at the disposal of the library, but the Syndics were in favour of using it for lecture-rooms, of which there was a most absurd and undignified shortage. This demand was backed up by the heavy guns of the Woodwardian Professor of Geology, the Norrisian Professor of Divinity, the Plumian and Jacksonian Professors of Philosophy, the Lucasian Professor of Mathematics, the Regius Professors of Physic, Greek and Modern History, and the Professors of Botany and Anatomy, all of whom had to play Box and Cox in such rooms as were available.

Finally it was decided to clear the whole site and erect an immense new building facing King's Parade which should house the library and satisfy all the homeless professors. This impressive decision was made in 1829. The architects Decimus Burton, Cockerell, Rickman and Wilkins were each asked to submit designs and the years rolled on and Cockerell's design was chosen. It was magnificent, in the grand Grecian manner, fully worthy of that great architect. But the destruction of Gibb's and Wright's work would have been a terribly heavy price to pay. This design was quarrelled with, amended and approved of again. Then the university discovered that it could not afford it. In the end, the Syndics recommended that only the north side of Cockerell's scheme be carried out ; which it was in 1840, and the effect from Senate House Passage is not pretty though the front is dignified. The west side, where King's Old Court had been, was added by Scott in 1863, incorporating as much as there had ever been of the old gate.

So through all these condemnations and reprieves the Old Schools and the Senate House survived.

In 1722 James Burrough prepared a design for the new Senate House, but James Gibbs (whom we have already met at King's) was officially appointed architect. The Syndics ordered that " Mr. James Gibbs do take with him to London Mr. Burrough's plan . . . and make what improvement he shall think necessary upon it." The result of this joint effort is what we see now, the most elegant and sophisticated piece of architecture in Cambridge, blandly and serenely putting to shame the monstrous Waterhouse block of Caius, which clearly it ignores as thoroughly as it ignores King's Chapel.

This very satisfactory addition was nearly finished by 1725, but only opened in 1730. Gibbs had intended it to be the north wing of a three-sided group, with a new library as the centre block, but, as usual, such violent controversy arose over details that the full plan was dropped. It was revived in 1752 when Burrough produced a revised version of Gibbs' design for the library front only, but this time the Chancellor, the Duke of Newcastle, intervened. As we have already seen, Newcastle was continually intervening in a very trying way. On this occasion he sent down drawings by his own favourite architect, Stephen Wright, together with £500 towards the cost. This blackmail was too strong for the Senate, who dutifully approved Wright's design. It was finished by 1758.

Although no one can claim that it matches the Senate House very well, this library front is a good façade. It is less graceful than its neighbour, but more masculine and therefore perhaps more suitable for a university town. The central window holds it together rather well, and heaviness is avoided by setting back the ends and carrying the projecting central part on a very nice arcade.

Cambridge is really uncommonly rewarding to the enthusiast for Georgian building. Not only has it the Senate House and the Gibbs or Fellows' Building at King's, which are famous and are in all the books on English architecture ; but it has the various buildings and courts by James Burrough at Peterhouse, Caius, and Trinity Hall, and by James Essex at Peterhouse, Queens', Emmanuel, and Trinity. It is, one gathers, customary to describe most of this as dull ; those who find it so presumably find any evidence of good manners dull and prefer the company of untidy and picturesque bohemians—which evidently is why so much of it is obscured and ruined by a straggle of creeper, which is flamboyantly colourful for a week or two in the autumn and dank and dreary for the rest of the year. The cool colour of a well-controlled wistaria does no violence to a Georgian ashlar front, and a little ivy is very proper on a romantic piece of *faux-Gothique*; but not Virginia creeper.

Cambridge being a place for the serious pursuit of knowledge, an academic and learned place, there is very little architecture of the purely fashionable kind; perhaps the Senate House is the nearest approach to the modish on a large scale, and the Gate of Honour at Caius is certainly modish in the allusive Elizabethan manner. But, in general, Cambridge building reflects not that which was for a time regarded as smart, but that which was at any particular moment accepted as correct: the Renaissance, the Palladian, the Classic, and the neo-Gothic are all in the most widely used idioms of their day (though the last two overlap), and, with the staggering exception of King's Chapel, there is very little in the way of adventure. Thus in the eighteenth century we do not find fashionable Chinesery or Strawberry Hill Gothick being used by the decorous Burrough or the well-tempered Essex; their work is always satisfying, never exciting. Neither of them is very original, certainly neither of them is a great master; but even the commonplace of the eighteenth century should make a strong appeal to us to-day, by its functional rightness and its clear-headedness. If Burrough sets out to design a range of chambers for gentlemen to live and study in, that exactly is what he designs. If Waterhouse sets out to do the same thing, God alone knows what is going on in his mind.

The last years of the Georgian age, which are the first years of the nineteenth century, produced Downing College, as remote from most of the other colleges in space as it is in time. Its nearest neighbour is Emmanuel and the gate leading to it is in St. Andrew's Street on the opposite side to Emmanuel and nearer the station.

The conception of Downing was peculiar, its birth difficult and much of its subsequent history unfortunate. Architecturally its youthful ambition was splendid and full of high promise, but the promise was only in part fulfilled and recent attempts to redeem it have not been too happy.

In 1717 a local magnate, Sir George Downing, made a will leaving estates in East Anglia in trust for certain relations and in due course for the founding of a college to bear his name. He died in 1749 and his cousin and heir died without issue in 1764. But Lady Downing, this cousin's widow, was still alive and flatly refused to give up the estates; the furious litigation which followed was cleverly kept alive by the lawyers for another thirty years.

But all this time the question of selecting a site went on being discussed. As usual, James Essex was in on it with some plans in

1771, but was, for a change, unsuccessful. James Wyatt, in 1784, wanted to build it on the Backs with four fine façades. George III, who was not ignorant of architectural problems, recommended that it might not be a Gothic building, which was very proper in so august a pupil of Sir William Chambers. In 1796 the trustees nearly bought the common known as Parker's Piece, behind the University Arms Hotel, and then went to the other end of the town and nearly bought a site on Castle Hill. Finally they bought the present site in 1804 and a good deal more; it was an immense area originally, and stretched from St. Andrew's Street nearly the whole length of Downing Street, to Tennis Court Road.

The previously disappointed James Wyatt was chosen as the architect and his plans were submitted by the Master to Mr. Thomas Hope of Deepdene, who then wielded in matters of taste an authority equal to that of Ruskin later. Mr. Hope disapproved, and Wyatt was disappointed once more. So then plans were obtained from Byfield, Wilkins and others, and in 1804 those of Wilkins were adopted. The uncompromisingly classical design is about as different as anything could be from the Gothic Wilkins we find in other colleges. It is his earliest appearance in Cambridge and started him on the career which the University so largely provided for him.

The college is built round a huge quadrangular space about as big as Trinity Great Court. In theory the effect should have been imposing, but in practice it is not quite as serene and impressive as it ought to be. The end porticoes are very good and have a great air of authority, but the rest is not up to their standard. By 1820 the west side was finished and part of the east, but after that nothing was done till the 1870s, when E. M. Barry completed the east side more or less in accordance with Wilkins's design. Early in the 1930's Sir Herbert Baker brought the college nearly to completion. His new buildings, at first sight, fit in fairly well; but not on a second look. They are full of the most unaccountable references to purely seventeenth-century mannerisms. The chapel whose site was laid out along the south side of the court, was never built, though the site was consecrated and a Fellow of the college, Sir Busick Harwood, was even buried in it, in 1814. It must be an unusual and lonely experience for a man to be buried in a chapel which does not exist. The completion of Downing is for our modern chapter.

Downing still has charmingly park-like immediate surroundings, but nothing to what it might have had. In the years after 1896, after a most unfortunate financial mishap, the college had to sell most of the land between the actual buildings and Downing Street;

the University bought it, and it is now wholly devoted to the cause of science, being covered with a multitude of laboratories and technical museums.

Downing is certainly rather disappointing, the more so as it contains some really admirable Regency, and might have been one of the best pieces of Grecian in England. Its character is, however, quite unmistakably late Georgian and on the whole it closes that great age pretty well. The real nineteenth-century Cambridge provides some very odd experiences and a few exciting ones.

XI Nineteenth-Century Cambridge

A N EXCURSION THROUGH THE NINETEENTH CENTURY IN CAM-
bridge entails, above all things, keeping one's head. It
begins decorously enough with Downing and the Regency,
but almost at once we are involved in the thick of the Battle of the
Styles, with the Classical fighting a losing campaign against the
Gothic. This Gothic question is a little complicated; first, of
course, one must forget about Sir James Burrough and even about
Sir Christopher Wren and Robert Grumbold; but if one really
wants to appreciate the flavour of *faux-Gothique* one ought to try
to ignore also the real mediæval, and this, in a place whose ines-
capable focal centre is King's Chapel, is a little difficult. Nevertheless, Cambridge neo-Gothic is not just a pastiche on the Middle Ages.
The lessons of symmetry and architectural planning taught by the
late seventeenth and eighteenth centuries were never really forgotten until Waterhouse fogged everyone's minds with his own
muddle-headedness.

Look, for example, at the Trumpington Street front of Corpus. The
accent is strong Gothic, but the language is classical; the façade is
absolutely symmetrical, and its rhythmic stresses are almost equally
divided between vertical and horizontal. Sidney Sussex seems at
first sight to be a mass of Gothic pinnacles, but it too is really a
classical form in a Gothic dress.

Nearly every college was active in building or rebuilding between
1820 and the 'seventies. We have already seen a good many of the
results, but there are a few important things we have not yet seen.

First of all, the New Buildings at St. John's. One's introduction to
this should be made from the lawn between Trinity Library and the
river, so that one's back is to the Library and the old buildings of
St. John's are screened by the willows. Seen thus, the New Building

71   Old Schools : the East Room

72   New University Library : the Royal Library of George I

73   St. John's : the New Buildings

74   St. John's : the "Bridge of Sighs"

75　King's : the Screen, from the Front Lawn

76　King's : Pinnacles on the Chapel Roof

78 St. John's : the Hall

77 King's : the Hall

is isolated and looks almost like a separate college, with no reference to anything else. It really is an astonishing experience; intrinsically, the building has real architectural qualities of a high order, but it depends on extrinsic factors even more. It insists on being looked at scenically and it succeeds.

Many people hate this court vehemently, many admire it extravagantly, but nobody can ignore it, any more than they can ignore King's Chapel or the New University Library. And it is no good trying to dismiss it as sham, because that is the one thing it is not. Had the architects merely tried to imitate the Stuart manner of the old buildings, that would indeed have been sham, but this romantic and blatantly sensational mass is entirely an expression of its own post-Byronic day. The architects were surely right in ignoring the rest of the college; that was complete (remember, the old chapel still existed) and the river must act as a frontier between that complete whole and any new buildings. By not attempting to imitate and by abandoning the original axial line, they not only emphasised the character and individuality of their own work, but preserved that of the old; it was left for Scott to destroy it.

The decision to build this fourth court across the river was arrived at in 1825. The chosen design was that of Thomas Rickman and his young partner Henry Hutchinson, and it was to be in red brick and to follow the plan of the famous second court. This was definitely laid down, so that the college must have been rather astonished to find itself with a huge, towering mass in the Perpendicular manner and stucco-fronted. If one stands in the great entrance and looks at the vaulted roof or walks along the vaulted cloister, one gets a good idea of the immense scale of the whole. The old and new are joined by a covered-in bridge, romantically called the Bridge of Sighs. This is not a very graceful object, but it has an awkward charm and a distinct air; and it does not attempt to refer itself to the exquisite Grumbold bridge or to that at Clare.

King's provides another good Gothic experience, of ten years earlier. Here once more we encounter our friend William Wilkins. He was a great man in his day, but the centenary of his death in 1939 was not very widely noticed; it was indeed hardly noticed at all. Wilkins had a curious professional career; as an undergraduate at Caius he took an extremely good mathematical degree and then got a Fellowship. Travels in Greece and Italy turned him to architecture, and at twenty-six he secured the commission to design Downing. For the next ten years he worked with great profit in correct and admirable Grecian and then suddenly, about 1814, went Gothic and built Dalmeny in Scotland. Rather more than ten years after that he reverted to the Grecian and built University College Gower Street. Downing was the beginning of Wilkins's career, but it was the Gothic building at King's that brought him full recognition.[1]

We have already seen how the building of King's stopped in the reign of Henry VIII, with the college consisting of the chapel and the Old Court to the north of its western end, and how the Fellows' Building was added by Gibbs. At last, in 1823, the college decided to plunge a little farther, and even more daringly, by building on land it had owned since about 1445. William Wilkins was the man it chose. He may have begun as a Grecian, and indeed had already designed the classical bridge across the river at Kings, which though plain and unassuming has excellent lines, but he had lately proved himself to be fully versed in the Gothic.

Wilkins' work consists of the main gate and the screen running right along the King's Parade front southwards from the chapel, and the very long stretch of buildings along the south side, or left as one enters, including the hall, a staircase of chambers and the Combination Room, the library, and the former Provost's Lodge. The screen is by far the best part; it is very charming and elegant in itself, and marries happily with the chapel, to which it manages to stand up very bravely. Here, as at Sidney Sussex and too many other colleges, there is an obscuring overgrowth of vegetation which wholly wrecks the design. Admittedly the spirit of the screen is romantic enough to demand a few tendrils of ivy, enough perhaps for one owl to hoot in by moonlight, but it does not deserve to be smothered.

Wilkins intended the inner side of this screen to have a cloister; he also intended to gothicise the Fellows' Building. Both of these schemes fell through, fortunately in the latter case; had the Gibbs building been third-rate its gothicising might have produced something quite pretty, like Bishopsthorpe at York. Since Gibbs is very far from third-rate it is a mercy that the scheme was abandoned. But the original drawings are extremely interesting all the same. The southern range is dull but sound, with nothing gimcrack about it, though the old Provost's Lodge is an admirable building, good Grecian inside and good Gothic outside. The interior of the hall is well worth seeing; Wilkins has avoided the temptation of imitating the traditional open roof, which later Gothic revivalists failed to resist, and his proportions are almost noble. Being by Wilkins, it is not usually given its due praise, but really it is one of the best of the larger college halls. It is quite rightly dominated by

[1] Gavin Walkley, *Country Life*, December 30th, 1939.

a whole-length portrait of Sir Robert Walpole, whose benefactions were so largely responsible for the new building by Gibbs. The two lanterns instead of the usual single one are rather unusual.

The rest of the college consists of Chetwynd and Webb's Courts behind the Wilkins range and Bodley's right at the western end down by the river ; also a small block of incredible gloom across the lane beyond Chetwynd, which is reached by a dank subterranean passage. Chetwynd is by Scott, built in 1871, and, although the outside facing the merging of King's Parade with Trumpington Street is not very memorable, the inside is rather charming : admittedly, the impact of this charm is not very immediate, but it grows.

Additions to the buildings of King's had become necessary after 1861, when the new Statutes initiated by the Royal Commission came into force. Till then, King's had consisted simply of seventy Etonians, Fellows and Scholars. Scott's new building was the first result, and at the same time two other projects were considered ; first, to buy the Bull Hotel, and secondly to pull down Wilkins' screen and build a range right along King's Parade. Designs were actually produced by Scott, again, and by Street (the architect of the Law Courts). Both these schemes faded out, but in 1879 the college, still yearning for *Lebensraum,* made overtures to St. Catharine's for a union of the two foundations. King's may have called this amalgamation, but small St. Catharine's certainly called it absorption and shrank from such an idea.

A part solution was found in 1889, when Bodley's Court was begun. Until its completion a few years ago it was two-sided. It has dignity and is picturesque without being tiresome ; it also has a charming position, to which it certainly owes much of its effect. Webb's Court, behind the hall and with a gate into Queens' Lane, was built in 1908 by Sir Aston Webb, who was much patronised by Edwardian Cambridge. During the late 1920's and early 1930's the new Provost's Lodge, with its entrance in Webb's, was devised. It does not particularly reflect any of the other buildings in style, but it harmonises well in the all-important matter of scale. The fountain in the middle of the Front Lawn, with its rather arch little statue of Henry VI, was designed by H. H. Armstead in 1879. It hardly does justice to the spirit of the founder, being a somewhat timid and pedestrian object.

Southwards from King's, past what was once the Bull Hotel, past Wilkins' Classic-Gothic Corpus, past St. Catharine's, and by the junction of Silver Street with Trumpington Street is a very noticeable piece of 1830 Gothic, the Pitt Press. It is by Edward Blore, and is an important object in the vista from the Fitzwilliam northwards

towards King's. The Press is not a bad building, and is a great
deal better than Blore's work at Lambeth Palace, which must add
an intolerable weight to the burden of being an archbishop.

The University Press has been established pretty well where it
now is since 1655, though the first press in Cambridge was set up by
John Siberch in 1521 and the first Charter authorising a University
printer was granted by Henry VIII in 1534. Since 1655 the Press
has always been somewhere in the area bounded by Silver Street,
Trumpington Street and Mill Lane and the acquisition of the actual
present site has been piecemeal, beginning in 1762. This mock-
collegiate front of Blore's was started in 1831 and owes its origin to
the admirers of the younger Pitt. The Pitt Club of London had
resolved in 1824 to erect the statue of Pitt in Hanover Square and had
decided to use any surplus funds for " the erection of a handsome and
appropriate building at Cambridge connected with the University
Press, to bear the name of Mr. Pitt." As an example of comparative
costs, it may be noted that Sir Francis Chantrey's statue cost over
£7,000 and Mr. Blore's building cost under £11,000.

Farther still along Trumpington Street, just beyond Peterhouse,
is the great classical front of the Fitzwilliam Museum. When Lord
Fitzwilliam died in 1816 his splendid bequest was at once handed
over to the university and a Syndicate was appointed to look after
it. It took them an unconscionable time to make up their minds
about a site for a suitable building. From 1816 till 1842 the collection was housed rather inconveniently in an otherwise disused part
of the Perse School, and from then till 1848 in part of the University
Library.

The Syndics began splendidly by asking King's to sell them the
whole of their King's Parade front, which at that time was not
built on. This request met with a firm rebuff. Then they asked
St. Catharine's to sell them the Bull Hotel, and met with another
rebuff. Then in 1823, after several other schemes had fallen through,
they persuaded Peterhouse to sell them part of the present site, and
were so delighted with this success that they did nothing more for
eleven years. In 1834 the Perse School announced that it wanted
the accommodation taken up by the collection, and although the
school did not get possession till eight years later, this jolted the
Syndics into doing something about a building. Their intention
was publicly announced, and the chief competitors were George
Basevi (rather oddly, Disraeli's uncle), James Pennethorne, Thomas
Rickman, Anthony Salvin, Lewis Vulliamy, and of course William
Wilkins. Basevi's design was chosen and the work was begun in
1837. It proceeded steadily but slowly till 1845, when Basevi fell

down the inside of the west tower of Ely Cathedral and was killed. The building was incomplete, and C. R. Cockerell was entrusted with the finishing of it; later still, E. M. Barry had a hand in the business, especially in the interior, and additions were made after the first world war which are among the best pieces of museum-architecture in the country.

The grandeur of the Fitzwilliam, with its great Roman portico, makes an immediate impact on the visitor driving from the station, if his taxi happens to take the Lensfield Road way instead of going along St. Andrew's Street past Emmanuel, and the promise of splendours to come is well redeemed a moment later by a distant glimpse of King's. The Fitzwilliam is the great monument to the memory of Basevi, as the Taylorian at Oxford is to Cockerell and the British Museum to Smirke; all three stout, stately, classical and all designed between 1823 and the end of the 'forties in the very thick of the Gothic revival.

The only other important relic of early nineteenth-century Cambridge building is Sidney Sussex. This is rather a long way and demands a taxi, especially as there nearly always is one outside the Fitzwilliam. If one walks, one returns past King's to Great St. Mary's or up the narrow and pleasant alley of St. Edward's Passage, in which one still finds David's famous enormous and incredibly untidy book-shop, across Market Hill (perfectly flat) to Holy Trinity, and along Sidney Street.

Sidney, as we have already seen, was first completed just before 1600 by Ralph Symons. At the beginning of the nineteenth century it was described as " a neat little brick building, with nothing in it remarkable." [1] About 1820 the college decided to make improvements which almost amounted to rebuilding, and adopted the plans proposed by Jeffry Wyatt. Wyatt, a member of the architectural dynasty of that name, was later magnified by George IV into Sir Jeffry Wyatville and is best known as the rebuilder of Windsor Castle; that, the large additional wing at Chatsworth, and Sidney Sussex are his best achievements.

The work at Sidney was begun in 1831. By his ingenious arrangement of the entrance and the two adjacent open courts, each court is entered from a corner, which, since they are quite small courts, is important, as it gives a view of the biggest possible extent. This not very eminent little college, though deplorably blurred with thick tangles of creeper, has a quite charming *faux-Gothique* character, and is much too romantical to permit any thoughts of Oliver Cromwell to obtrude themselves. The mercilessly neo-Renaissance Chapel

[1] Dyer's *Cambridge*, 1814. Quoted by Willis and Clark.

is, however, more generally admired. While the two courts are a
translation of Gothic into the current idiom of the 1820's, the chapel
is an elaborate and careful imitation, by T. H. Lyon, of an Italian
style which was emphatically not the current idiom of the 1920's; it
would have been much better to have left Essex's chapel of 1780,
which firmly spoke its own language and did not try to imitate
anything else. However, it looks very rich and costly.

Nearly opposite Sidney is the entrance to Whewell's Court, which
is part of Trinity and leads through to Trinity Street opposite the
main gate of the college. We have already spent a good deal of
time at Trinity, but since we are looking at early nineteenth-century
buildings we may as well see what that heterogeneous college can
provide.

Whewell's courts have, as a series, a depressing effect, though the
eastern one makes a brave effort with a few flowers and some neat
grass. They were built by Anthony Salvin, the one nearest Trinity
Street in 1859, when Dr. Whewell, Master of Trinity, was alive and
supervising it, the remainder soon after his death in 1866.

In the south-east corner of the Great Court a passage leads
through to a small, unsuspected court, very Wilkinsish, packed in
between the back of the Great Court east range and the backs of
the shops in Trinity Street. The student of Wilkinsiana will find
this stucco castellated-Gothic not unrewarding. The main side of it
is pretty in a whimsical, Castle-Wilkins manner, though the setting
is dreary; it is dated 1834.

But the most important nineteenth-century addition to Trinity is
Wilkins's New Court, alternatively called King's Court, which is
adjacent to Nevile's Court, to the south. There are three entrances,
one from Bishop's Hostel at the end of Trinity Lane; one opposite
this, which opens on to the avenue of newly planted limes leading to
the river and Essex's bridge (there are very few views in Cambridge
which can beat this); and the third which leads from Nevile's Court.
New Court, which was begun in 1823, is not generally approved of
and is thought dull, but it is all the same a very distinguished piece
of Wilkins. Arthur Hallam kept in this court when it was still
quite new, and it is safe to assume that the memory of it stayed
with Tennyson till his death—how lucky for Tennyson that Hallam
could never have kept in Whewell's.

Before we leave the epoch of Wilkins, who served Cambridge on
the whole pretty well (though perhaps not so well as Cambridge
served him), we might make the pilgrimage to Lensfield Road, which
runs into Trumpington Street at the point where stands the fanciful
Jacobean Hobson's Conduit. At the corner of Lensfield Road and

80　Pembroke : Buildings by Waterhouse

79　The Pitt Press

81 Downing (from Ackermann's *Cambridge*)

82 Sidney Sussex : the Chapel Court

83   The Fitzwilliam Museum

84   The Fitzwilliam Museum : the Main Hall, from an Engraving of *ca.* 1840

85   Dinner in Hall

Panton Street, embowered in trees and shrubs, is the house Wilkins built for himself; a neat and pleasant Regency villa, with nothing whatever of Gothic about it. It later housed the University Appointments Board. There are some attractive terraces of houses on the far side of Parker's Piece which may also be examples of Wilkins's almost-Grecian domestic style.

We need not detain ourselves long over the rest of the nineteenth century. Ruskin and Butterfield did not impress their mark on Cambridge as they did on Oxford, and Waterhouse, who in the Natural History Museum in Kensington showed himself a serious architect of considerable powers, merely wrought irreparable harm at Caius and Pembroke, though he did produce quite a good building at Jesus. But an architect who did do some important work at Cambridge was G. F. Bodley. We have already noticed his chapel at Queens'; here opposite Jesus he designed the best of Cambridge's many Victorian parish churches. This is All Saints', a building which replaced the mediæval church, of the same dedication, which long stood in the triangle of ground across Trinity Street from the chapel and great gate of Trinity. The new church in Jesus Lane, with its irregularly spaced windows and a really fine tower and spire placed unusually far to the East of the building, was started in 1863 and finished in the next year; it has some bells, a font, and some memorial tablets from the original All Saints'. More important are its excellent, though now much faded interior decorations by some of the pre-Raphaelites. The East window contains panels from designs by Morris, Burne Jones, and Madox Brown, while the painting of the walls and roof is by members of the same school. All Saints' and its neighbour Jesus Chapel are the chief places in Cambridge for pre-Raphaelite studies. The 'seventies and 'eighties produced the usual crop of revivalist *compôtes* and the 'nineties and early 1900's tried to get back to something a little more architectural, without a great deal of success. Once past Scott Gothic, we are mostly regaled with a diet of pink brick Jacobethan and the stone-fronted Edwardian Renaissance. Another really fine Victorian church is the Roman Catholic one of Our Lady and the English Martyrs which one passes on the way up from the station. It was finished in 1890 and is in Decorated Gothic, with a slightly French feeling in its apsidal sanctuary and in the elaborately flamboyant organ gallery. It has a pair of western transepts, and at its North-West corner a tower with a graceful spire which is modelled on that at St. Mary's, Oxford. Not far from this church the Anglican St. Paul's, opened in 1842, has a brick and stone West tower which is a very respectable rendering of East Anglican Perpendicular.

Before embarking on this, there is a pleasant *hors d'œuvre* in the classical portico of the Pitt Club,[1] a little way down Jesus Lane on the left. All this corner-site in Jesus Lane and Bridge Street was formerly the Hoop Inn, which comes into Wordsworth's *Prelude* ; part of the admirable early Georgian front may still be seen in Bridge Street above a garage and motor-shop, and the little A.D.C. Theatre[2] occupies the old Assembly Room, up Park Street off Jesus Lane. Before the A.D.C. occupied these tucked-away premises they housed the Union Society, which was founded in 1814 and moved there in 1832. In 1866 the Union moved to its present building behind the Round Church, which was built for it by Waterhouse. It is typical Waterhouse, full of references to all sorts of styles, but even its Waterhouse character has been destroyed by a wholly characterless internal reconstruction. The Hoop existed until 1910, but the coach-yard in Jesus Lane was sold in 1853 and a Turkish bath was built on it ; this in turn was sold in 1865 to Sir Matthew Digby Wyatt and leased by him to the Pitt Club, who moved in at once. This Wyatt, like Sir Jeffry Wyatville, was a member of the Wyatt dynasty, and designed Addenbrooke's Hospital. He was also the first Slade Professor of Fine Art in Cambridge. It is believed that either he or his brother, T. H. Wyatt, designed the portico for the bath and the present club reading-room, which was originally the cold plunge. Although the club has been much altered, the portico has survived. It is a charming toy in 1850-classical, and seems to speak out from its motor-and-cycle shop surroundings with greater authority than it really carries.

Near the corner of Market and St. Andrew's Streets, next to Holy Trinity Church, is a very singular piece of Dissenters' Gothic built in the mid-1880's by Professor Prior. It is the Henry Martyn Hall, headquarters of the University Church Missionary Society. The ecclesiastical effect is a little marred by the ground-floor being occupied by part of an extensive furnishing shop, whose show-window is cramped inaptly into the gothic frame.

The 'seventies and 'eighties produced the three colleges which though in the University were not originally a part of it. Girton, completed in 1873, and Newnham, opened in 1875, the two women's colleges ; and Selwyn, founded in 1882. Girton is by Waterhouse and provides rich material for keen students of his vagaries ; it is mostly in brick Law-Courts Gothic, but has a Tudorish Gate to show that it is really in Cambridge. Newnham is by Basil Champneys and is a riot of revivalist Tudor, full of picturesque nooks and oriels

---

[1] See " The University Pitt Club," by W. M. and C. M. Fletcher, 1935.
[2] See pp. 98–99.

and gables ; it is one of the buildings in Cambridge which really would benefit by being covered with ivy, wistaria, magnolia, jasmine and every kind of creeper. Champneys also designed, in 1876, the fanciful red-brick building opposite the Gate of St. John's, the Selwyn Divinity School. It has all his characteristics of fussy borrowed detail and an apparent inability to know when to stop.

Selwyn, built by Arthur Blomfield, is a rather different matter. It is designed deliberately in the manner of Ralph Symons, with the second court of St. John's in mind, but adapted to nineteenth-century college requirements. The buildings are therefore much taller than anything Symons ever built, but Blomfield showed considerable and unexpected restraint in keeping them fairly plain. When the college was opened it was right in the country and cattle grazed in the fields that separated it from Newnham. The bland and well-to-do Bedford Park-ish suburb that occupies all the western part of Cambridge beyond the Backs was only developed between then and about 1905.

XII   Modern Cambridge

DESPITE MANY DIFFERENCES IN THEIR PAST HISTORY AND IN THE emphasis now placed on their various studies, there is much resemblance between our two ancient Universities. There is far less between the busy, largely industrialised City of Oxford and the county-town which is Cambridge.

Large numbers of tourists visit Cambridge, though they are fewer than those who go to Oxford. But when a visitor does reach Cambridge, everything is made beautifully easy for him, speaking geographically.

The classical grandeur of the Fitzwilliam Museum makes a good initial impression, and he then proceeds straight along the narrow main artery known successively as Trumpington Street, King's Parade, Trinity Street and St. John's Street. He passes in turn Peterhouse, Pembroke, St. Catharine's, Corpus, King's, Caius, Trinity and John's. An unrivalled procession, dominated in the middle by King's Chapel and ending with the great Tudor gateways of Trinity and John's. He will then get into a punt and move slowly upstream in the quiet beauty of the Backs, the most perfect man-made view in England. The great overhanging willow by the Wren Library, the river-front of Clare, the great lawn and meadow of King's, the red brick of Queens' and John's rising straight from their own reflections in the river, are things which no Cambridge man can ever forget until he dies.

The stranger will see them and will envy the young men and women who spend three years in this beauty. He will perhaps try to learn something more about the character and peculiarities of the place, and he may not get very far. He will learn that a man's

Some of the matter in this chapter may still be more true of the years between the wars than of the 1950s. But I have not ventured to say much on the period since the 1930s when my own continuous personal experience of Cambridge ended. As Mr. Steegman has rightly seen (see the preface to the 4th edition), there have been many changes at Cambridge since his time and mine.—B.D.G.L.

rooms are looked after by a woman known as a " bedder ", that food in some college halls is indifferent, but that some college kitchens can produce ravishing meals for private parties, that a quadrangle (including those that are three-sided) is called a court, and that honours examinations are called triposes. He will find, or could in the 1930's, that a man or woman is perfectly at liberty to work when and how he or she pleases, but that they are by no means at liberty to do no work at all. Discipline, as exercised by the Tutor in College or by the Proctor outside, is firm though never rigid, while a man can get drunk if he wants to, with authority generally holding the view that the next day's hangover is sufficient punishment.

Pursuing his enquiries into the different colleges, the stranger will find that Jesus and Trinity Hall have traditionally tended, in recent decades, to produce rowing-blues ; the latter of these two colleges has also upheld its fine legal tradition. Pembroke has produced rugger-blues and poets, and Caius its medical students. Trinity has a very distinguished record in classics, philosophy, and mathematics, is vast and heterogeneous, and used to contain many of the rich young men who hunted, went to Newmarket, rode in the Cottenham point-to-point, and were determined to aim at nothing higher than a pass-degree. King's, moreover, has tended to be different from everywhere else, this difference being a matter for frowns and head-shaking on the part of other colleges, and self-congratulation on the part of Kingsmen.

There are several clubs, though not so many as at Oxford. The Pitt, which is social, rather exclusive, and elegant ; the absurdly named Athenæum, which once was largely composed of rich Etonians and Wykehamists and the hunting crowd ; the Hawks, which is athletic ; the Union, to which every male member of the University can belong, which exists both for debates and as a social rendezvous, and which has been a nursery for Primy Ministers ; the political clubs ; and the dramatic clubs—the A.D.C., the Marlowe, the Footlights, and others.

The Marlowe has had a distinguished career, being founded by a group of men including Rupert Brooke to perform the more difficult and lesser-known Elizabethan plays ; it is well thought of, if at one time rather overloaded with a number of perennially youthful dons. The Footlights performs admirable home-made revue in May-Week and was the nursery of Jack Hulbert. The A.D.C. corresponds to the O.U.D.S. of Oxford, but does not have to engage professional actresses, being content to rely on the wealth of talent to be found among the dons' widows, wives and daughters.

There was another, less officially recognised, club ; barely perhaps

a club, more a fraternity—the Night-Climbers.[1]   Since at least the
1870's the pastime of climbing by night up the towers and
pinnacles and across the roofs has been popular and, necessarily,
furtive—guide-books, anonymously published, have described the
Trinity Kitchen Plateau, the Drain-Pipe Chimney in St. John's New
Court, the severe Chetwynd Crack in King's, the very dangerous
N.E. Spire Traverse on King's Chapel or the classic Sunken Drain-
Pipe on the Old Schools.[2]   All of them romantic, hazardous climbs,
where the reward of success was a circumscribed and private glory
and the penalty of failure was being either crippled or sent-down.
More widely practised were the more or less nursery climbs into
colleges from outside by belated undergraduates, where to fail was
to be disembowelled on revolving spikes and to succeed was merely to
avoid being gated.   Another aspect of these activities is seen in the
heavy bills, sometimes running into several hundreds, that have to be
paid by colleges repairing the superficial damage so caused to their
buildings.

Athletics and politics are indulged in by most young men at both
the universities.   The extreme cultivation of both activities is
indulged in by minorities, which are always noisy and which, suffering
from the arrested development which is the heritage of English
youth, bring with them the habits and *clichés* of the school playing-
field and debating-society.   They have a brief and very pleasant
authority at Lord's, Twickenham, Putney or in the Union, and
are soon forgotten.   Undergraduate politics are not a matter of
great importance or interest, and it is sheer nonsense to regard the
Union debates as being barometers of opinion.   Young men tend
to the left in politics if they are gifted with eloquence, and to the
right if they are not.   The man who speaks in the Cambridge Union,
even if he be the Foreign Secretary specially asked up from Whitehall,
can be fairly certain that nobody outside the debating-room will
pay much attention to anything he says.   The Oxford Union differs
in that there the words of even a freshman, at least in the 1930's, were
apt to be reported by a large section of the Press.

Modern Cambridge has produced not unworthy successors to its
greatest men in earlier centuries.   Balfour, the philosopher-
statesman, succeeds Bacon ; Inge succeeds the Cambridge Platonists ;
Rutherford succeeds Newton ; Housman carried on the poetic
tradition; McTaggart that of the pure philosophers.   And the
prominent and distinguished intellectual coterie which was given the

---

[1] *The Night-Climbers of Cambridge*, by " Whipplesnaith," Chatto and Windus,
1937 and 1952.

[2] See *The Cambridge Review*, June 9th, 1937.

86   In the Backs

87   Punt in Progress

88   Punts for Hire

89   Clare : the New Buildings

90   The New University Library

91　Trumpington Street from below Peterhouse

92　St. John's, the Future

regional designation of " Bloomsbury " is by origin a Cambridge movement : the Cambridge of the Stephens, the Keyneses, the Bells, and Roger Fry. But Cambridge is not unduly concerned with those whose names make or have made news or with praising of famous men simply because they are her sons.

In two fields, very different from each other and ones in which until recent times the University was not always pre-eminent, there have been astonishing developments, of significance far beyond Cambridge. And both are concerned primarily and ultimately with teaching. The two fields in question are those of music and science.

The Professorship of Music [1] actually dates from 1684, but only within our own times has it been placed on the same footing as all the other professorships. The progress of muscial research, the enterprise in performing rare and unknown works, and the increase in the number of music students have caused, since about 1900, a development in musical scholarship and in the art of musical appreciation which now makes Cambridge a really important music centre famous from Vienna to Harvard. Cambridge woke up to the importance of recognising " music " as a gentleman's profession in 1893, for the first time since the seventeenth century, when degrees were conferred on Tchaikovsky, Saint-Saëns, Boito and Bruch. That was a tremendous occasion. Then the German musical world was astonished by a performance in 1910 of Marlowe's *Faustus* with the then quite new idea of contemporary incidental music. But the performance that has had the loudest repercussions was that of *The Magic Flute* in 1911, in English. The *Flute* was till then a completely forgotten opera, and its present popularity dates from that performance at Cambridge. Since then much important work has been done by the Cambridge University Musical Society (C.U.M.S.), and musicians like Boris Ord of King's have done much to add to the musical lustre of the University.

Stanford and his successors in the Chair of Music were not, unfortunately, at first imitated by the Slade Professors of Fine Arts. Yet in the Fitzwilliam Cambridge has one of the most important collections in the country, and it can, if intelligently used, play a great part in helping students with a first-class knowledge of European history, languages, and literature to appreciate that they still have an incomplete experience if they remain ignorant of the fine arts. How, for example, can an undergraduate hope to understand anything real about Dante if he has never heard of Giotto ? Or appreciate seventeenth-century intellectual life if he has never encountered

---

[1] See *Groves' Dictionary of Music*, under " Cambridge."

Poussin ? One great and important exception to an earlier tendency was in the field of English mediæval studies ; the learning in this that emanated from St. John's was based on a deep knowledge of the social aspect of architecture and painting, and had a marked effect on mediæval studies. Now, moreover, the general attitude of Cambridge has considerably altered, and the Slade Professors have had a far greater and more receptive following than in the earlier years of this century.

The aim of Cambridge teaching is not to show young men a quick route to success and not primarily to train them for a specific type of job. Roger Ascham in the sixteenth century pleaded for the endowment of research, and Cambridge has ever since been well satisfied to train men in the way of learning, in the knowledge that men with minds tuned to the habits of systematic scholarship can be relied on to repay their debt by good service to society in later life. The avowed careerist will probably find Cambridge unsympathetic to his ambitions, and the impatient man had better cut out the place altogether and go straight to a training-school or a business-house.

The Cambridge method is brilliantly illustrated in the systematic study of medicine under Clifford Allbutt, physiology under Michael Foster, physics under Thomson and Rutherford, astronomy under Eddington and music under Dent. These men have shared two great qualities as teachers—a profound knowledge of the history of their subject and a gift for picking out younger men who can succeed them as teachers.

The history of the Cavendish Laboratory is in large measure the history of modern physics in England. Its achievements have been reached by a tradition, and the tradition has been formed by a succession of men unknown to the outer world, inspired by great leadership, and content to work for the common cause of learning rather than for their own personal renown. The Cavendish Laboratory is certainly not the only place in England where this tradition is followed, but it is there that it has been illustrated with particular success. The system really is founded on the distinction between teaching and cramming or forcing. Which is why, if asked to name a typical Cambridge man of the last half-century, one would say Sir Michael Foster : by no means the greatest physiologist of his day, but far and away the greatest teacher of physiology.

All of which leads up to the question of what Cambridge is *for*. In the 1920's heads of businesses when taking new men on to their staffs used to reject those with a Cambridge or Oxford degree—in the belief that they had been wasting three years of their life. In the 1930's they began to think that the man with a good degree probably had a good brain which could equally well be adapted to wool, railways, brewing or advertising. That is certainly not always true, but it is more nearly so than to think of the university years as a waste of time.

What is Cambridge for ? Not primarily to give a man the degree of B.A., as he can get that at other Universities and will have to work harder for it probably ; not, certainly, to enable him to proceed M.A., since that, happily, can be done by simply paying a fee instead of having to sweat for two years over a thesis. This is one of the few pieces of privilege which is left to us, and only a prig would sanctimoniously deplore that a Cambridge M.A. degree, which is bought, has a far greater prestige than a London one, which is worked for.

Prestige still does not altogether answer the question, though it partly does. Cambridge is really for those who want to go there. The reason may be snobbish, and to have such a wish may be a sign of improvidence, but there still are parents who feel that their sons can benefit by three years of mixing with other people's sons on terms of friendship governed by the conventions of a world that is no longer schoolboy and not yet fully adult, conventions that have taken some centuries to evolve and which are designed for the undergraduate and not for his critics ; for succeeding generations of young men who are, for the first time, young men, who a few minutes ago were schoolboys and in a few minutes more will be men with responsibilities and all the cares and anxieties of a competitive world.

For three years the undergraduate can be as serious or as inconsequent as he likes, though if he persistently flout authority he will be sent down. But there is at least an even chance that in those three years he will acquire a standard of values which may make for happiness and may give him a balance between leisure and endeavour in his professional life later on.

The English youth takes rather a long time to grow up, longer than the French, German or Italian adolescent, and there is a good deal to be said for a system which enables a youth to devote three years to the process and emerge at the end of it an educated man. But the parent who sends his son up to Cambridge must be quite clear about the meaning of " education " ; he must realise that in these days it is something of a luxury, since one of the things it does not mean is " to train for a specific job or occupation." Among the things it does mean are " to form habits, manners, mental and physical aptitudes " ; " systematic instruction in preparation for the work of life " and " the culture or development of powers and the formation of character." [1]   These are luxuries, if a parent wishes his son to make up his mind about a job the minute he leaves school, that is to say before he has a mind to make up.   But the University will endow him with a mind, with " mental aptitudes," and will if he is at all educable teach him how to apply his mind to the work of life ; it will not try to teach him primarily how to apply his mind to the work of being a barrister, an engineer, a doctor or a civil servant, and he will have to begin doing that in earnest when he comes down ; when he does begin, he will do so with a more mature and better-filled mind than those possessed by his competitors who have been forced, and whose faculties have been canalised, since they were seventeen.

One point however arises that specially affects modern Cambridge. In the field of science instruction is given which can be, and indeed generally is, actual training for a specific profession, so that the man who goes up and studies, say, physiology or physics is studying those sciences in the place above all others equipped to teach him. That is a very good reason for going up to Cambridge instead of to anywhere else, if you are going to be a physiologist or a physicist.

Yet in general it is still true to say that knowledge gained at the University, and perhaps in particular that gained at Oxford and Cambridge which have had many centuries in which to evolve their traditions and social life, has this advantage over knowledge acquired at a crammer's or in an office—it is not only wider but also more enduring.

[1] *Shorter Oxford English Dictionary.*

XIII Modern Architecture in Cambridge

IT MUST BE PECULIARLY DIFFICULT TO DESIGN A NEW BUILDING in Cambridge for either town or gown. But it is a difficulty that obviously has existed for quite a long time now, and has had to be faced by Symons and Grumbold, Essex, Wilkins, and Waterhouse. The first faced it by building in the newest modes of his day, which had evolved quite naturally and logically from what was already there. In 1602 the second court of St. John's was modern, but its buildings were in style not radically different from the fourteenth-century Corpus; they were only rather grander. Grumbold and Essex faced the problem by building in the correct modes of their days, which had not evolved out of anything in England, but had been imported. In 1680 and 1780 Clare and the south-west block of Queens' respectively were modern, and no attempt was made to harmonise them with their neighbours. A correct architect was so certain of his rightness that it would hardly occur to him to revive something which may have been all right once, but was so no longer. Wilkins set the fashion for revivals, but whether he were reviving Greek or Gothic he always spoke with authority. Downing, Trinity and King's are not only scholarly, but also direct, and they state their purpose perfectly simply. So does Blore's Pitt Press despite its modern re-fenestration.

Cockerell, whose only equal in the nineteenth century is Charles Barry, no more had need to bother about fitting himself in with something else than had Wren. Both Trinity Library when it was new and the Fitzwilliam Museum when it was nearly finished silenced criticism by at once assuming the dominant authority that they have exercised ever since.

Then it all went, and during the last thirty or forty years of the century, the age of Waterhouse, Basil Champneys, and the ponderously learned Sir T. G. Jackson, there was no longer any authority, certainty or directness. One kind of revival succeeds another, and as often as not two or three kinds are muddled up together in one group, as at Waterhouse's Pembroke or Champneys' Newnham. Sometimes a style is introduced that never existed in Cambridge at all, like Waterhouse's German Schloss at Caius.

The end of the century and the beginning of the Edwardian age mark the reign of Sir T. G. Jackson. The Downing Street–Pembroke Street area is his kingdom, lying between Pembroke and Emmanuel and bounded by Tennis Court Road on one side and Free-School Lane on the other. Not that it is all built by him, but it is all very Jacksonian. Its great characteristic is opulent heaviness, with an extraordinary mixture of Edwardian vulgarity and undigested learning. Sir T. G. Jackson certainly knew a High Renaissance building when he saw one, and that was his favourite style. So he set to work to produce amorphous masses covered with Renaissance detail, which perfectly illustrate the difference between mannerism and style.

This extraordinarily depressing area is one of the most intense concentrations of scientific knowledge in England. It includes the Cavendish Laboratory in Free-School Lane, for the cost of which the seventh Duke of Devonshire was personally responsible, and has produced all the achievements in physics, biochemistry, biology and physiology which give Cambridge its unchallenged leadership in scientific research. But nobody would imagine, if he did not already know, that these meaningless shapes are really laboratories and museums which draw students and scholars from over the whole world. They might be banking-houses or the dwellings of Edwardian millionaires or liberal clubs.

Besides the Cavendish Laboratory of Experimental Physics, there are in this immediate neighbourhood the Marshall Library of Economics, the Chemical, Zoological, Pathological, Physiological and Mond Laboratories, the Institutes of Parasitology and Biochemistry, the buildings for Psychology, Medicine, Surgery, Human Anatomy, Genetics, Botany, Agriculture, Economics and Geography, and the Museums of Geology, Archæology and Ethnology, Medicine, Mineralogy and Petrology, and Zoology. Addenbrooke's Hospital is the southern boundary, and just beyond that are the Engineering Laboratories and the Department of Aeronautics. The head swims as one enters this sacred region. Some of the temples were opened in 1904 by King Edward and Queen Alexandra, and probably most of the spectators got more satisfaction from contemplating the lovely and unlearned queen than from the learned and unlovely buildings.

There are, however, one or two of these institutions which do not actually hurt the critical spectator. The Humphry Museum and Medical School is a most interesting piece of 1904 modernism designed by Professor Prior in a style which still seems agreeably simple and free from mannerism. The Zoological Laboratory, built in 1934 by Mr. Murray Easton, does at least look like a laboratory and tries to be neither picturesque nor stylish, whereas the Marshall Library, built by Sir T. G. Jackson on the south side of Downing Street, tries hard with its lantern, arches, dormers and five long fancy windows to be both. The Institute of Biochemistry in Tennis Court Road, designed by Sir Edwin Cooper in 1923, is exceedingly stylish, though what style it is supposed to be is not certain, nor can one be certain when looking at the outside as to what function this very self-conscious pink-and-white edifice is intended to perform. Just beyond it is the excellent building of the Department of Pathology. This, designed in 1926 by Mr. Edward Warren, has distinct Queen Anne references, but they are adapted with great intelligence to the actual and present facts. It is a really happy marriage between the traditional-humanistic and the modern-functional.

During the 1914–18 war plenty of people predicted that Cambridge could not possibly survive, yet in the years after that war the numbers increased to such an extent that several colleges had to build either new wings to existing buildings or new courts altogether.

Magdalene, for instance, in 1909 had given itself a block by Sir Aston Webb on the river bank beyond the library, which is sober, inoffensive and not in the least memorable. About 1925 it had to extend again. This time it crossed the street and erected the Benson Court, designed by Sir Edwin Lutyens. Even second-rate Lutyens has an air about it, and this court is certainly not first-rate Lutyens. The façade is too long to be able to dispense with some kind of central feature, but it is not an ill-bred building, if rather commonplace. Its construction involved the demolition of Fisher Row, a small wharf with picturesque little houses and cottages. This was the last but one of the hythes which in the Middle Ages lay along both banks of the river for the unloading of barges coming up from King's Lynn, and was much beloved by water-colourists who, on its destruction, would willingly have flung their camp-stools at Sir Edwin. Still, they ought to be satisfied with some equally ancient houses whose fronts are opposite the main entrance to Magdalene ; these originally formed the Cross Keys Inn, and the inn-yard is now the entrance to Benson Court. Next to Benson is

Mallory Court, all gables and whitewash, which has recently been not so much designed as contrived. It is very artistic.

Across the river from Magdalene, and towards the Union, are the additions to St. John's, designed by Edward Maufe. On the way notice the iron Great Bridge, which was built in 1823 and is by no means ungraceful. Just by the bridge is a particularly ludicrous piece of Olde-worlde in the shape of a Jacobethan motor-shop and garage, which even the things on the Great West Road could hardly beat.

The newest court of St. John's, which was finished shortly after the start of the second World War, really is rather peculiar. It is certainly worthy of a great college, and does something to redeem the crying sins of the Chapel. But for three irritating features it would not only be an admirable but a very attractive building; in its actual design it is admittedly logical in relation to the alignment of Bridge Street, and also in relation to the Chapel, whose scale and character have been very carefully considered by the architect. The three annoying features are the convex side wings, which not only curve for no apparent reason, but also bear a most awkward relation to Bridge Street, the fenestration, which includes those disagreeable, long, narrow strips which run right down the face at intervals, like fire-escape ladders, and a little adjunct, much lower than the rest of the court; it projects from it towards St. John's Street at a right angle, and runs into the main building with an inconsiderate bump. Still this court and the new court at Clare are the best additions made in the period between the wars to Cambridge college architecture. Another important group of buildings of this period is to be found at Jesus, in the range of staircases which completed Chapel Court. The work was finished in 1930, and the architect was Morley Horder who had already designed the plesantly neo-Gothic Cheshunt College at the other end of Cambridge and had done some lesser work in Jesus itself. The style, which does not at first sight seem very original, is closely modelled on one of the versions of late Perpendicular in which Bishop Alcock had remodelled the buildings he took over from St. Radegund's Priory. Ever since the seventeenth century it had been the consistent practice in Jesus to model new buildings more or less closely on the college as Alcock's designers had left it; even Waterhouse had followed this practice, which is why his building at Jesus is so much less unmannerly than his other Cambridge perpetrations. So this latest of the college's buildings was in fact built in accordance with a tradition which it would have been illbred to disregard. His sculpture is important, for a large shield of arms (they are those of Bishop White-Thompson of Ely), and its two angel supporters, are by Eric Gill.

93   Downing: the Court as finished, 1953

94   Christ's: one of the New Blocks

95   The Cam, looking to St. John's from Trinity

96   The Cam, looking to Trinity Bridge

97 Crocuses in the Backs

(before the limes were felled and replaced by new trees)

98 The Cam, looking to King's and Clare Bridges

At the other end of the town is Queens', whose newest block, by G. C. Drinkwater, is across the river. The façade is curved, but not content with that, which simply handled might have been very effective, the architect has introduced a number of unexplained and unrelated features which certainly avoid the commonplace but do not avoid the vulgar.

Not far from Queens', Peterhouse erected, in 1939–40, another of the more important Cambridge buildings of this period. Known as Fen Court, and designed by Mr. H. C. Hughes, it is built in a considerably more contemporary style than is most modern collegiate architecture in Cambridge, and its unusual shape in a way foreshadows that of the post-war Garden Hostel of King's.

Caius is about half-way between Bridge Street and Silver Street. Its new court, St. Michael's, was begun in 1904 by Sir Aston Webb and lies around the little church across the street from the repellent Waterhouse building. The extension beyond, facing Market Hill, is not very attractive. It looks, for the moment, exceedingly modern and will therefore quite soon look exceedingly dated. Seen from the Market, the staring white front catches the eye violently but having caught it gives it no real satisfaction. It is like a platitude which is delivered as a strikingly original remark.

The new Guildhall on the other side of Market Hill is neither a platitude nor particularly original, but it has certain positive merits. For some reason, it is fashionable in Cambridge to disparage this good building. Since the Market Hill is a hopeless muddle of commercial offices, shops and cinemas, it calls for something with authority to dominate it, which the eastern aspect of Great St. Mary's just fails to do. The Guildhall is a very big, rather stark mass taking up the whole south side of Market Hill, and carries its bulk with dignity, partly because of good proportions and partly because of very good fenestration. The yellowish-grey stock-bricks are ugly, but they are the local vernacular of the Eastern Midlands and are well suited to a Cambridge town building. It was built in 1938 and replaces the familiar old 1859 Guildhall, which was in comfortable Mid-Victorian classical taste. A new County Hall in neo-Renaissance stock brick and stone, had already been completed on Castle Hill.

Since Market Hill is the centre of the town, as opposed to the University, the new block of Caius becomes in part a town building, and as such it is much less successful than the Guildhall. Cambridge is not a modern, industrial city, and Market Hill and the east side of Trinity Street–King's Parade have the air of a country town, with snippets of everything and nothing violent or sudden. There is the much-restored Elizabethan house between Trinity and Caius, on the opposite side, which is now a café ; there is the charming Georgian front next to it, which now houses a famous bookshop, and there are several pleasant, solid, sedate early nineteenth-century houses, especially in King's Parade, built in the local brick. These combine to form the character of the town, and the Guildhall, despite its size, fits into this picture very well.

Walking due west from Market Hill, across King's Parade, down Senate House Passage, through Clare, over the bridge, along the avenue and on to the other side of the Backs Road, we enter the presence of the most controversial building Cambridge has had for generations : the New University Library, which stands behind and towers above the new buildings of Clare. Both these are by Sir Giles Gilbert Scott, the library 1931–34 and Clare five or six years earlier. One belongs to the University, the other to a college, and they are entirely distinct and separate from each other. Yet it is difficult not to think of them as together forming one composition in two movements.

In Clare Sir Giles has produced something quite worthy of his reputation. It consists mainly of two modern-classic wings of nice proportions, with a central feature that contains the entrance-arch. And it is that which almost succeeds in lowering the dignity of the rest by the unnecessarily fanciful arrangement of the gates within the arch. It is difficult to be charitable about this feature, but it does not seriously affect the rest of the court. Very rightly, there is no hint of nor reference to the old court, from which it is separated by the river, the avenue and the thickly-wooded Backs.

The New Library has caused a lot of trouble since its completion. To begin with, it has administered a violent shock to the Cambridge centre of gravity. Hitherto, that has traditionally been in the group formed by the Old Schools, the Senate House, King's Chapel and the University Church of St. Mary. The University Library is by its nature the cathedral of intellectual life, and the old site was the physical as well as the intellectual centre. The new site implies a new focal point across the river and widely separated from the rest of the University.[1] That in itself was something of a disturbance, but the actual buildings are even more disturbing, for they have changed the whole balance of the panorama.

The main cause of trouble is the tower. Not only is it an un-beautiful object in itself, but there is by no means general agreement on the necessity of a tower at all. It is placed in the centre of the

[1] This situation will be much altered by the gradual development of the Sidgwick Avenue site.—B.D.G.L.

façade and thereby destroys the composition of the rest, and it also breaks up the architectural relation of the Library with Clare. With the tower placed at one end of the façade the trouble would be lessened, and with the tower left out altogether it would be lessened even more. But there would still remain the long, narrow windows, running up from ground to cornice. These windows are bad enough in the new block at St. John's, where they do at least indicate staircases, but here, in a building which is not designed on the collegiate staircase system, they give the effect of a warehouse. In a sense, perhaps, a library is a kind of warehouse. But in a University Library some observance of tradition and some reference to the Humanities might be not altogether out of place.

The interior looks, and doubtless was, very costly. A pathetic attempt to establish continuity between the old and the new has been made by fitting up in the east gallery some of the elegant bookpresses from the west room of the old Library. It has the opposite effect, for this is the only spot which suggests scholarship as opposed to instruction.

Cambridge did not at first take kindly to its New Library. Still taste performs its curious revolutions, which generally take about a century. Caius is due to be much admired by the *avantgardists* of some twenty or thirty years hence, and perhaps the Library will come into its own around the year 2020.[1]

Since 1945 Cambridge has had some large, useful, and socially important additions to her college and University architecture. To some extent these reflect a present-day life, and perhaps foreshadow a future, in which the returning visitor will notice marked differences from the Cambridge of the years between the wars. The emphasis on science and engineering is as great as ever, and this is shown by the " priority " given to new buildings for the training of engineers and chemists. The main course of University life itself is more subtle, more elusive, more difficult to sense unless one is oneself a resident member of the University. At first, one is told of the years immediately after 1945, it seemed that many of the old ways and attitudes of mind had perished beyond recall in the holocaust of war and social change. It is certainly true that, with the economic revolution and the prevalence of Ministry of Education grants, the undergraduate population is differently composed, and in a way has a different outlook, than was the case with many who came up before 1939. It is also important that many of those who now come up to Cambridge have already done their National Service ; the undergraduate body is on the average older than it has usually been. Yet

---

[1] The remainder of this chapter is by the reviser.—Publishers.

DESCRIPTION

it is noticeable, now that the great post-war influx has disappeared, and with it some of the fantastic congestion which then made Cambridge a bedlam and lodgings a fable, that many of the old traditions and ways have strongly reasserted themselves. So the Cambridge of the 1950's seems, to one now revisiting it, a less unfamiliar place than it did six years ago. The ways of Cambridge are ancient and very deep by the roots. Tradition, once it is old and firm enough, becomes a more durable force than social innovation or deliberate change.

Yet one does find changes, albeit some of them may be considered as changes of degree and not of kind. In many colleges, or at least in many college buildings whose internal arrangements allow it, the occupation both of a " keeping " room and a sleeping room has given way to living in a single " bed-sitter " with a gas or electric fire. One eats far less in one's own rooms than was once the case. At least in the newest accommodation, which tends in some colleges to be more popular than the old buildings, it is now less of an expedition to one's bath. Moreover, the difficulty in getting lodgings has led several colleges, by means of new buildings (as in Downing, Christ's, and others) or by the intelligent conversion of existing sets (as in Jesus) to increase the number of their men who live in.

Of the completely new college buildings the most important are in Downing, for here is not merely the addition of a range but the completion, round three sides of its great campus-like court, of a college. The gap between Sir Herbert Baker's two blocks has been filled by a range whose Ionic portico is closer in style to Sir Herbert's pillars than to those of Wilkins. The range itself is simpler than Sir Herbert's work of the early 1930s, and lacks the " Queen Anne " features which are incongruous amid a scene of generally Grecian purity. The designer was Mr. A. T. Scott, and the building was put up in 1951–53. Most of it consists of living quarters, but behind the central portico is the chapel, not on the site where Sir Busick Harwood was hopefully buried, but here at the northern end of the court, its " eastern " end projecting from the main bulk of the new range. It has a severe, unadorned, Romanesque-feeling sanctuary, while the woodwork of its screen and stalls is reminiscent rather of the time when Sir George Downing made his will than of the period of Wilkins.

From Downing one goes up St. Andrew's Street, past the University Arms, past Emmanuel, and so to Christ's where two important new blocks have been finished, one of them in 1950, the other in the autumn of 1953. Both are wholly residential, and together they are an important addition to the college, both for their style and as a

112

means of housing about ninety men. Their architect was Professor A. E. Richardson, and their style, with a creamy facing of Ketton stone, is a severe, perhaps over-lofty, four-storeyed rendering of the late Georgian tradition.

So across Cambridge to the Backs, and past Trinity Hall where another building has been put up to Professor Richardson's designs. The Bursary Block, finished in 1951, is small, pleasant, not very college-like (it partly consists of offices), or dynamic in its character. Yet it performs good service by completing and defining a new court between the college's mediæval buildings and Garret Hostel Lane. The chief feature of this court is the more or less unaltered back of the main court's northern side, and here the mediævalist can happily forget the staidly Palladian transformation wrought by Burrough upon the principal court of the college founded by Bateman and built in the main before the fourteenth century was out.

Standing in ground taken out of the area of the Fellows' garden, the Garden Hostel of King's, designed by Mr. Geddes Hyslop, is perhaps the most interesting, and certainly the most thoughtfully decorated of Cambridge's new college buildings ; it was finished in 1949.[1]

Being a separate hostel, and not an element in a court, it does not need to conform, and does not conform, to the usual system of " staircases " in a rectangular block. Though not a revolutionary building, and though it has neo-Adam features to embellish its pleasingly red brick walls, it is more contemporary in its style than post-war blocks in the actual colleges have so far ventured to be. Inside, it has " bed-sitters," and a breakfast room which makes unnecessary a long trek across the Backs to breakfast in hall ; the room has curtains made to designs by Graham Sutherland. The main external feature is a tower (which was to have been higher), and beneath it a stairway leads up to the corridors of rooms. On the stairway, and along the corridors, are mural decorations in which Bloomsbury has repaid a few pennies of its cultural debt to Cambridge. For tiled panels, depicting flowers and still-life designs and in one case a lushly Baroque deity, have been made from designs by Duncan Grant and by Quentin and Vanessa Bell. A happier touch, and one most worthy of so great and historic a college, is in the bronze newels at the bottom of the stairway. For there, embedded in the heads of the newels, are two coins, a penny of 1949 and a groat of Henry VI.

[1] For this Hostel, see the *Architect and Building News*, February 16th, 1951.— B.D.G.L.

Not far from this hostel, on the other side of a site for which an important future is planned, the new entrance lodge of Newnham is tamely William and Mary. Luckily it is dated 1949, so that there is no risk, in future ages, of its being taken for a building 250 years its senior.

One hears also of new projects, or of more buildings actually started by various colleges. Clare are making a small addition, one presumes in the Scott manner, to one side of their Memorial Court. Trinity, already responsible for a hostel in the gloomy canyon of Green Street, are to build a new block down by the river, on the site of their brewhouse and in the corner between the Cam and Garret Hostel Lane. In such a position, and as an addition to the architecture of the Backs, it cannot fail to be important, just as one cannot disregard Mr. Frank Lloyd Wright's proposed contribution to the architectural make-up of the Grand Canal. Trinity College is here putting itself under a great responsibility to the future.

The University, with a great building programme, has so far been more venturesome in style than the colleges, which seem to have found it less easy to build in a contemporary vein than did foundations like Christ's and Trinity (but not Jesus, Queens' and Pembroke) in the seventeenth century. The Health Centre at Fenner's, and the lofty new Engineering Laboratory between Coe Fen and Trumpington Street, are both of them buildings of obviously twentieth-century design. Of the two, the Engineering Laboratory is the more remarkable and bulks high, with its rectangular shape, above the other buildings which lie between Addenbrooke's and the Leys. At the present time, in Lensfield Road, it is getting an equally bulky neighbour in a block which will house a large number of chemistry laboratories.

More important, and even more than the New University Library betokening a shift, from central to western Cambridge, of the centre of academic gravity, are the schemes now made public for a great " precinct " of University buildings in the almost empty space between Sidgwick Avenue and West Road. Cambridge, with its central area insolubly congested, was indeed courageous when the New Library was built so far away from the Old Schools. Now the tendency so started is to be pushed very much further, in particular for the students of the Humanities, for whose benefit nearly all the new accommodation is planned. The architects who have produced the scheme are Sir Hugh Casson and Mr. Neville Conder. They have done little more than give the general scale and outline of the buildings whose erection they propose. Yet it is not surprising that one envisages a general effect, with allowances for the per-

manency of the buildings, which one might not unfairly designate as
" South Bank." The site is level, and almost virgin. Its designers
are free, with no neighbours more architecturally respectable than
Newnham, Selwyn, and Ridley Hall, to work in as contemporary a
manner as they may have at their fingers' tips. As Sir Hugh Casson
says, " the architecture of the surrounding buildings sets no stylistic
theme which it would be ill-mannered to ignore." They do, however, allow for some vistas on to Selwyn, and for a considerably more
important one from one of their courts to the tower of the University
Library. Yet they do not, so far, give us any elevations whereby
one may compare their notions with the work of Symons, the Grumbolds, Gibbs, Wilkins, or even Waterhouse. Apart from the sugges-
tion that a good many buildings may be supported on " stilts," so
that one may then be able to promenade beneath them as one can
below the Royal Festival Hall, or as one could in 1749 beneath the
Radcliffe Library at Oxford, one is now left in the main to consider
the nature and the grouping of the buildings proposed.

Many activities are to be grouped here, all of them in one way or
another connected with the " Arts " ; I do not know what is due to
happen to the present Arts School or to the neo-Georgian block of
lecture rooms which was finished, in the 1930s, in Mill Lane. Lecture
rooms, faculty libraries, a Music School, " seminar rooms," and the
Museums of Classical Archæology and of Archæology and Ethnology
are all in time to be accommodated on the site. Three Assembly
Halls are suggested for largely attended lectures such as those now
delivered on Greek tragedy by the Provost of King's or on artistic
matters by the Slade Professor of Fine Art. The architects propose
that their buildings should be grouped round a series of loosely connected courts. One of these is to contain a large square pool of water ;
one hopes that it will, if placed in such an academic setting, be less
infested with the baser urban débris than is a similar feature outside
the new Council House at Bristol. Large lawns are suggested " for
contemplation," and many existing trees would be left standing up
and down the precinct. A facing of stone is planned for the " serene
and timeless " blocks like large lecture halls and the haunts of the
more numerous faculties ; the other buildings would in such a case
be content with an exterior of brick.

So great a scheme as this cannot be carried out in one operation,
and several phases are expected before all is complete. One cannot
at the moment say exactly when work will start, or how soon the
earliest blocks, whether gauntly rectangular or making more con-
cessions to a sense of outline and adornment, will be completed.
Nor can one be sure, in a place where such a matter may well be hotly

debated before a decision comes, of the precise style in which the elevations of the buildings will be carried out. One thing is certain. If the Sidgwick Avenue site is built upon as the University proposes it will comprise Cambridge's most important academic building for many years. It may even be architecturally exciting.

Index

The numbers in *heavy* type denote the *figure numbers* of illustrations.

INDEX

INDEX

INDEX